NINJUTSU
HISTORY AND TRADITION

NINJUTSU

HISTORY AND TRADITION

DISCLAIMER

Please note that the publisher of this instructional book is NOT RESPONSIBLE in any manner whatsoever for any injury which may occur by reading and/or following the instructions herein.

It is essential that before following any of the activities, physical or otherwise, herein described, the reader or readers should first consult his or her physician for advice on whether or not the reader or readers should embark on the physical activity described herein. Since the physical activities described herein may be too sophisticated in nature, it is *essential that a physician be consulted.*

UNIQUE PUBLICATIONS

265 S. ANITA DR. STE. 120 ORANGE, CA 92868

©**UNIQUE PUBLICATIONS INC., 1981**

Printed in the United States of America
First Printing
ISBN: 0-86568-027-2
Library of Congress No.: 81-70819

Design by Jeff Dungfelder   Daniel M. Furuya: Editor

Dr. Masaaki Hatsumi
34th Grandmaster of the Togakure Ryu

DEDICATION

I have had in this lifetime the rare fortune to have encountered a divinely inspired warrior sage. This book then is dedicated to the master teacher Toshitsugu Takamatsu, as an expression of my gratitude for all that he gave me.

ACKNOWLEDGMENT

This book would not have been possible without the cooperation and encouragement of my student, Shidoshi Stephen K. Hayes, and blooming in the shadows, the kunoichi Rumiko. May happiness last forever for them, and may their family continue to grow and expand in health, prosperity, and understanding. It is my prayer that this book of ours will make even a small contribution towards deepening the friendship between the nations and people of Japan and the United States.

ABOUT THE AUTHOR

Dr. Masaaki Hatsumi was born in Noda City, Chiba Prefecture on December 2, 1931. He graduated from Meiji University in Tokyo, with a major in theater studies, and now is the director of his own chiropractic clinic in Noda City.

In the 1950s and 1960s, Dr. Hatsumi continuously travelled across Japan to study with Toshitsugu Takamatsu, of Kashiwara City, Nara Prefecture, from whom he received his initiation into the life ways of the ninja. The author later inherited from his teacher the authority and position of headmaster in the following Japanese martial traditions:

34th Soke of Togakure ryu ninjutsu, originally founded by Daisuke Togakure

28th Soke of Gyokko ryu koshijutsu, originally founded by Hakuunsai Tozawa

28th Soke of Kukishin ryu happo hikenjutsu, originally founded by Izumo Kanja Yoshiteru

26th Soke of Shinden fudo ryu dakentaijutsu, originally founded by Izumo Kanja Yoshiteru

18th Soke of Koto ryu koppojutsu, originally founded by Sandayu Momochi

18th Soke of Gikan ryu koppojutsu, originally founded by Sonyu Hangan Gikanbo, lord of Kawachi

17th Soke of Takagi yoshin ryu jutaijutsu, originally founded by Oriuemon Shigenobu Takagi

14th Soke of Kumogakure ryu ninpo, originally founded by Heinaizaemon Ienaga Iga, who adopted the name Kumogakure Hoshi

Now retired from active teaching, Dr. Masaaki Hatsumi no longer accepts new personal students. He supervises the Bushinkan ("Warrior God Training Hall") organization, made up of his students who now carry shihan and shidoshi instructor titles and carry out the teaching work on a world wide basis.

AUTHOR'S PREFACE

I believe that ninpo, the higher order of ninjutsu, should be offered to the world as a guiding influence for all martial artists. The physical and spiritual survival methods eventually immortalized by Japan's ninja were in fact one of the sources of Japanese martial arts. Without complete and total training in all aspects of the combative arts, today's martial artist cannot hope to progress any further than mere proficiency in the limited set of muscular skills that make up his or her training system. Personal enlightenment can only come about through total immersion in the martial tradition as a way of living. By experiencing the confrontation of danger, the transcendence of fear or injury or death, and a working knowledge of individual personal powers and limitations, the practitioner of ninjutsu can gain the strength and invincibility that permit enjoyment of the flowers moving in the wind, appreciation of the love of others, and contentment with the presence of peace in society.

The attainment of this enlightenment is characterized by the development of the *jihi no kokoro,* or "benevolent heart." Stronger than love itself, the benevolent heart is capable of encompassing all that constitutes universal justice and all that finds expression in the unfolding of the universal scheme. Born of the insight attained from repeated exposure to the very brink between life and death, ninpo's benevolent heart is the key to finding harmony and understanding in the realms of the spiritual and natural material worlds.

After so many generations of obscurity in the shadowy recesses of history, the life philosophy of the ninja is now once again emerging, because once again, it is the time in human destiny in which ninpo is needed. May peace prevail so that mankind may continue to grow and evolve into the next great plateau.

Dr. Masaaki Hatsumi
34th Grandmaster of Togakure Ryu

THE ESSENCE OF NINJUTSU

A ninja popularity boom has been developing in Japan over the past decades, and the public has been flooded with movie, TV, and paperback novel ninja characters. Almost exclusively, the ninja have been portrayed as overlooking all concepts of right and wrong and all morality in order to accomplish their self-serving aims. Recent trends in the Western world have also attempted to portray the ninja as mere technicians of violence who feel justified in supporting any cause for the right amount of money or power. From polar extremes of the political spectrum, mercenaries and terrorists alike enjoy claiming a kinship to the netherworld ninja heroes of feudal Japan as depicted in the popular media.

None of these concepts comes anywhere close to the real ninja. Uninformed writers and self-promoting entertainers have merely used the art of ninjutsu to cater to audiences seeking the exotic and unusual. I must say that there is really nothing wrong with the entertainment industry bending the lore of the ninja to fit the demands of the public. However, it is a little surprising that Japanese and American audiences would believe that the weakly-researched flights of fancy of fiction writers were the true essence of ninjutsu. It is even more amazing, and a little amusing, that after awhile, the writers and entertainers become recognized as ninja authorities, and soon, anxious followers are busy billing themselves as actual practitioners of ninjutsu. This is happening in Japan, and I am told by my students in America that it is also taking place in the West.

Nin-po Ik-kan
The vow, "The law of the ninja is our primary inspiration!" followed by a bow, and the knowledge continues on its transmission to a new generation of *shinobi* warriors. Shinobi is another Japanese pronounciation for ninja.

1

As a service to those in the western world who seek knowledge of ninjutsu, I have compiled this book, based on my experience as the thirty-fourth headmaster of the Togakure ryu ninja tradition. I inherited the title of *soke*, or head of the family, from Toshitsugu Takamatsu, the thirty-third headmaster of this style. My teacher was the grandson of Shinryuken Masamitsu Toda, the thirty-second *soke* of Togakure ryu. Behind us, eight centuries of history and tradition stretch all the way back to the founder of our system, Daisuke Nishina of Togakure Village. After defeat at the hands of Heike troops, Daisuke escaped from his birthplace in Nagano and took up residence in the remote region of Iga. There, he took on the name Daisuke Togakure, and later was credited with founding the Togakure ryu of ninjutsu.

The lineage of our headmasters is as follows:

Mo-ko, "Mongolian Tiger," as he was nicknamed by the Chinese boxers with whom he studied in his early 20s, Toshitsugu Takamatsu, the 33rd *soke* of Toga jure ryu.

1. Daisuke Togakure
2. Shima Kosanta Minamoto no Kanesada
3. Goro Togakure
4. Kosanta Togakure
5. Kisanta Koga
6. Tomoharu Kaneko
7. Ryuho Togakure
8. Gakuun Togakure
9. Koseki Kido
10. Tenryu Iga
11. Rihei Ueno
12. Senri Ueno
13. Manjiro Ueno
14. Saburo Iizuka
15. Goro Sawada
16. Ippei Ozaru
17. Hachiro Kimata
18. Heizaemon Kataoka
19. Ugenta Mori
20. Gobei Toda

While many would believe that the secrets of ninjutsu slowly vanished with the growing strength of the Tokugawa Shogunate, during the 17th century, or were buried under the closing of World War II, my teacher knew that the core truth of the *shinobi* arts would live on forever. The full significance of the wisdom of my teacher's teachers and their teachers can be seen in the late Toshitsugu Takamatsu's essay on the essence of ninjutsu.

"The essence of all martial arts and military strategies is self-protection and the prevention of danger. Ninjutsu epitomizes the fullest concept of self-protection through martial training in that the ninja art deals with the protection of not only the physical body, but the mind and spirit as well. The way of the ninja is the way of enduring, surviving, and prevailing over all that would destroy one. More than merely delivering strikes and slashes, and deeper in significance than the simple out-witting of an enemy; ninjutsu is the way of attaining that which we need while making the world a better place. The skill of the ninja is the art of winning.

"In the beginning study of any combative martial art, proper motivation is crucial. Without the proper frame of mind, continuous exposure to fighting techniques can lead to ruin instead of self-development. But this fact is not different from any other beneficial practice in life carried to extremes. Medical science is dedicated to the betterment of health and the relief of suffering, and yet the misuse of drugs and the exultation of the physician's skills can lead people to a state where an individual's health is no longer within his or her personal control. A nutritious well-balanced diet works to keep a person alive, vital, and healthy, but grossly over-eating, over-drinking, or taking in too many chemicals is a sure way to poison the body. Governments are established to oversee the harmonious interworking of all parts of society, but when the rulers become greedy, hungry for power, or lacking in wisdom, the country is subjected to needless wars, disorder, or civil and economic chaos. A religion, when based on faith developed through experience, a broad and questing mind, and an unflagging pursuit of universal understanding, is of inspiration and comfort to people. Once a religion loses its original focus, however, it becomes a deadly thing with which to deceive, control, and tax the people through the manipulation of their beliefs and fears. It is the same with the martial arts. The skills of self-protection, which should provide a feeling of inner peace and security for the martial artist, so often develop without a balance in the personality and lead the lesser martial artist into warped realms of unceasing

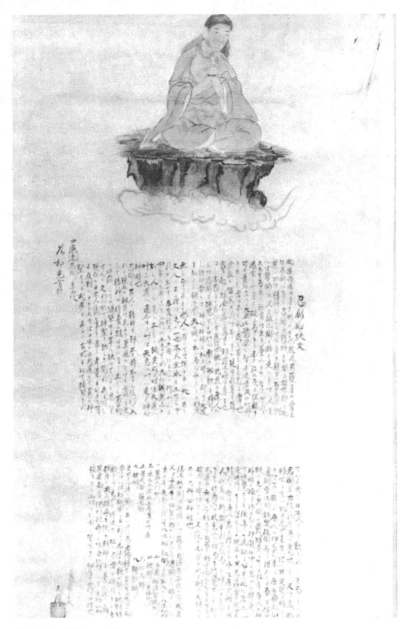

Ninjutsu Hiketsu Bun
This hand-written scroll by Togakure ryu ninjutsu, 33rd grandmaster, Toshitsugu Takamatsu contains the author's, teacher's views on the essence of the ninja art.

4

conflict and competition which eventually consume him.

"If an expert in the fighting arts sincerely pursues the essence of ninjutsu, devoid of the influence of the ego's desires, the student will progressively come to realize the ultimate secret for becoming invincible —the attainment of the 'mind and eyes of god.' The combatant who would win must be in harmony with the scheme of totality, and must be guided by an intuitive knowledge of the playing out of fate. In tune with the providence of heaven and the impartial justice of nature, and following a clear and pure heart full of trust in the inevitable, the ninja captures the insight that will guide him successfully into battle when he must conquer and conceal himself protectively from hostility when he must acquiesce. The vast universe, beautiful in its coldly impersonal totality, contains all that we call good and bad, all the answers for all the paradoxes we see around us. By opening his eyes and his mind, the ninja can responsively follow the subtle seasons and reasons of heaven, changing just as change is necessary, adapting always, so that in the end there is no such thing as surprise for the ninja."

— Toshitsugu Takamatsu

THE HISTORICAL NINJA

There are many theories as to the beginnings of what we know as the art of ninjutsu today. Each Japanese historian has his or her own set of facts and beliefs, and it is difficult pinpointing a specific place, person, time, or set of circumstances that would be acceptable to all as the birth of the art. In all truthfulness, ninjutsu did not come into being as a specific well-defined art in the first place, and many centuries passed before ninjutsu was established as a independent system of knowledge in its own right. The people who were later referred to as ninja did not originally use that label for themselves. They considered themselves to be merely practitioners of political, religious, and military strategies that were cultural opposites of the conventional outlooks of the times. Ninjutsu developed as a highly illegal counter culture to the ruling samurai elite, and for this reason alone, the origins of the art were shrouded by centuries of mystery, concealment, and deliberate confusion of history.

In the legends of the founding of Japan's Imperial Family, passed on by word of mouth through the generations before recorded history, two ninja-like characters are credited with assisting the first emperor, Jimmu, in attaining a decisive victory. Jimmu was in combat against the troops of Iso Castle, and the battle was going against him. One night in a dream, the future emperor had a vision in which he was told to take the clay from Mt. Amakaga and mold it into a sacred vessel. Mt. Amakaga was a holy mountain that lay in the middle of the territory held by the Iso forces. Obtaining the raw clay became the

symbol of Jimmu's intention and resolve towards succeeding in the conquest of Iso Castle. Shinetsuhiko and Otokashi served their lord Jimmu by disguising themselves as an old peasant and his wife, and the two successfully slipped into the enemy territory, packed the clay, and returned safely. Jimmu then molded and fired a platter and bowl set from clay, offered them to the gods of fortune, and went on to attain the victory he so strongly believed to be his destiny. The skills of ninjutsu were said to have been passed thereafter to Tennin Nichimei, Okume Mei, and Otomo Uji for further development and expansion.

Among the ancient ninjutsu documents that I inherited from my teacher are several scrolls that tell of Chinese ex-patriots who fled their native land to seek sanctuary in the islands of Japan. Chinese warriors, scholars, and monks alike made the journey to find new lives in the wilderness of Ise and Kii south of the capitals in Nara and then Kyoto. Taoist sages like Gamon, Garyu, Kain, and Unryu, and generals from T'ang China such as Cho Gyokko, Ikai, and Cho Busho brought with them the knowledge that had accumulated over the centuries in their native land. Military strategies, religious philosophies, folklore, cultural concepts, medical practices, and a generally wide scope of perspective that blended the wisdom of China with that of India, Tibet, Eastern Europe, and Southeast Asia were their gifts to their newly-found followers in Japan. Remote and far flung from the Emperor's court in the capital, the cultural ancestors of the ninja lived their lives as naturalists and mystics, while the mainstream of society became increasingly structured, ranked, stylized, and eventually tightly controlled.

As the passage of time continued to unfold the fabric of Japan's history, the ninja and their ways of accomplishment, known as ninjutsu, were always present behind the scenes working subtly with the events of all the eras to ensure the survival and independence of their families and lands. In the regions of Iga and Koga, ninjutsu became a special skill, refined and perfected by over seventy families, each with their own unique methods, motivations, and ideals.

Japanese history books, however, are curiously limited in their coverage and acknowledgment of the shadowy figures known as ninja. In textbooks even as recent as one generation ago, Hanzo Hattori, the head of one of the most influential ninja families in Iga and Shogun Ieyasu Tokugawa's director of ninja, was referred to as "a *bushi* (samurai) from the remote province of Iga." This hesitancy to openly acknowledge the ninja's role in the forging of modern Japan stems perhaps from the glorification of the samurai concept and ethic that became very popular after the Meiji Restoration (1868). The Meiji Restoration abolished the samurai class and gave all citizens the right to affect social trappings that had once been reserved for samurai only.

Map showing the many clans and family domains that were all embroiled in fierce civil war during Japan's Warring States period. The *shinobi* arts of stealth and endurance found many applications during this restless period of history.

Sengoku-jidai Warring States period battle tactics; a castle under siege. (From the author's private collection.)

With this clouding of significant historical events and people, it is difficult for today's Japanese people to understand the true purpose and ideals of the ninja. Exaggerated legends left over from the Tokugawa era, in which the Shogun's ninja secret police were given supernatural powers such as the ability to disappear, walk across water, and read minds, confuse the story even more. As the world became more and more interested in the culture and then the martial arts of Japan, the distorted stories of the ninja found new audiences in the Western world over the past three decades.

Even the words to describe the mystical shadow warrior art cannot be translated directly into languages foreign to Japan. *Nin* of *ninjutsu* and *ninja*, a single simple sound in Japanese, requires extensive English words to be explained. At its most elementary level, *nin* (also pronounced *shinobi*) can mean endurance, perseverance, and forbearance in both the physical and mental realms. *Nin* has a second dictionary definition of stealth, secretness, or concealment. The Japanese ideogram for *nin* is (忍), which is composed of the lesser ideograms of (刀) for "blade," and (心) for "heart." The construction of the written character implies that the heart, or will, is channeled and directed in ways that give it the effectiveness of the blade as a tool for accomplishment. In this broader sense of the concept, *nin* really means to be in control of one's body, mind, and perception of right and wrong.

It is easy to at least discuss being in control of one's body, and it has become quite fashionable in the West to discuss personal responsi-

Iga ryu ninjutsu leader, Hanzo Hattori, advisor to Shogun Ieyasu Tokugawa.

The village of Ueno in the province of Iga, from a woodblock printed by Hiroshige during the peaceful age following the Tokugawa unification of Japan. (From the author's private collection.)

Wreathed in smoke, Dr. Hatsumi weaves his fingers into the *"Rin"* position of the *Kuji-in* energy-channeling hand entwining series, stressed in the ninja's system of *seishin teki kyoyo*, spiritual refinement.

bility in the control of one's mind and emotions, but being in control of one's perception of right and wrong, or what is appropriate, is a more difficult matter. To be in control of one's perception of appropriateness is to be able to rely on one's "sixth sense" and to have a working knowledge of one's subconscious level of thinking. This broader perception of reality being based on one's own unique viewpoint is what set the ninja apart from the conventional military tacticians during the warring states and feudal eras of Japan.

The Togakure ryu, established approximately eight hundred years ago, is now in its thirty-fourth generation. The *ryu* (style) exists today as an organization dedicated to teaching effective methods of self-protection and promoting the self-development and awareness of its members. Due to the stabilized nature of contemporary Japanese government and judicial systems, the Togakure ninja ryu no longer involves itself directly in combat or espionage work. Previous to the unification of Japan during the 16th century; however, it was necessary for Togakure ninja to operate out of south central Iga Province. At the height of the historical ninja period, the clan's ninja operatives were trained in eighteen fundamental areas of expertise, beginning with this "psychic purity" and progressing through a vast range of physical and mental skills.

The eighteen levels of training were as follows:

1. SEISHIN TEKI KYOYO (spiritual refinement)

The Togakure ninja worked at developing a deep and accurate knowledge of himself, his personal power, his strengths and weaknesses, and his influence on the playing out of life. The ninja had to be very clear about his intentions, his commitments, and his personal motivations in life. Personality traits could often mean the difference between life and death in his line of work. Exercises in mental endurance, ways of looking at things, and proper perspective when evaluating things, were taught to the ninja along with his physical skills. By evolving into a mystic's understanding of the universal process, the historical Togakure ryu ninja became a warrior philosopher. His engagements in combat were then motivated by love or reverence, and not by the mere thrill of violent danger or need for money.

2. TAI JUTSU (unarmed combat)

Skills of *daken-taijutsu* or striking, kicking, and blocking; *jutaijutsu* or grappling, choking and escaping the holds of others, and *taihenjutsu* or silent movement, rolling, leaping, and tumbling assisted the Togakure ninja in life-threatening, defensive situations.

3. NINJA KEN (ninja sword)

The ninja's sword had a short straight single edged blade, and was considered to be his primary fighting tool. Two distinct sword skills were required of the ninja. "Fast draw" techniques centered around drawing the sword and cutting as a simultaneous defensive or attacking action. "Fencing" skills used the drawn sword in technique clashes with armed attackers.

The ninja's *taijutsu* as a means of dealing with multiple attackers.

13

The ninja's *kenjutsu* system for sword combat utilized a unique short bladed sword.

4. BO-JUTSU (stick and staff fighting)

The Japanese stick fighting art, practiced by samurai and peasants alike, was also a strong skill of the ninja. Togakure ninja were taught to use the *bo* long staff (six feet) and *hanbo* "half-staff" cane (three feet), as well as sticks and clubs of varying lengths. Specially constructed *shinobi-zue* or ninja canes were designed to look like normal walking sticks, but concealed blades, chains, or darts that could be used against an enemy.

5. SHURIKEN-JUTSU (throwing blades)

Throwing blades were carried in concealed pockets and used as harrassing weapons. The Togakure ryu used a special four-pointed throwing star called a *senban shuriken*, which was constructed from a thin steel plate. The blade was thrown with a flat spinning motion and hit its target with a sawing effect. *Bo shuriken* or straight shaft darts and spikes were also constructed for throwing.

6. YARI-JUTSU (spear fighting)

Togakure ryu ninja agents were taught to use standard Japanese spears and lances as middle-range fighting weapons. Spears and lances were used for stabbing and piercing attacks, and rarely ever thrown in normal combat. The Togakure ryu also used a unique spear weapon called a *kama-yari*, or "sickle lance," which consisted of a spear blade with a hook at the base. The total length of the weapon was over nine feet. The lance point could be used to lunge and stab, and the hook point could be used to snag and pull the opponent or his weapon.

7. NAGINATA-JUTSU (halberd fighting)

Virtually a short sword blade mounted on a long handle, the Japanese halberd was used for cutting and slashing attacks against adversaries at medium range. Togakure ryu ninja warriors were also proficient with the *bisen-to*, a huge heavy-bladed verion of the naginata halberd. Based on a Chinese war tool, the broad-bladed weapon was heavy enough to knock down attackers, smash through armor, and ground the horses of mounted samurai.

9. KUSARI-GAMA (chain and sickle weapon)

The Japanese chain and sickle weapon was adopted into the arsenal of the Togakure ryu ninja. A chain, six to nine feet in length and weighted at one end, was attached to the handle of the traditional grain cutting tool. The chain could be used to block or ensare the enemy's weapon, and the blade then used to finish off the attacker. The *kyoketsu-shoge*, a weapon similar to the chain and sickle, was favored by the Togakure ryu. The weapon consisted of a straight hand-held dagger blade with a secondary blade hooking out from the hilt, attached to a fifteen foot resilient cord usually made from women's or horse's hair. A large steel ring was attached to the free end of the cord.

9. KAYAKU-JUTSU (fire and explosives)

Ninja were experts in the effective placement, timing, and rigging of explosive devices for demolition and distraction. In later years, the use of black powders and other explosives was supplimented with

Bojutsu or staff fighting was one of the fundamental combat skills of all feudal age Japanese, commoner and samurai alike.

knowledge of firearms and their strategic applications.

10. HENSO-JUTSU (disguise and impersonation)

Essential to the ninja's espionage work was his ability to assume false identities and move undetected through his area of operation. More than merely putting on a costume, ninjutsu's disguise system involved thoroughly impersonating the character adopted. Personality traits, areas of knowledge, and body dynamics of the identity assumed were ingrained in the ninja's way of thinking and reacting. He or she literally became the new personality, whether taking the role of a monk, craftsman, or wandering entertainer.

11. SHINOBI-IRI (stealth and entering methods)

The ninja's techniques of silent movement, breaking and entering, and gaining access to inaccessible areas became legends in feudal Japan. Togakure ryu ninja learned special walking and running methods for covering long distances, passing over floors silently, and for staying in the shadows while moving, in order to facilitate entry and escape.

12. BA-JUTSU (horsemanship)

Togakure ryu ninja were taught to be proficient on horseback, both in riding and mounted combat skills.

13. SUI-REN (water training)

Stealth swimming, silent movement through water, methods of using special boats and floats to cross over water, and underwater combat techniques were taught to Togakure ryu ninja.

Throwing the card-like four pointed *senban shuriken* in a horizontal fashion.

14. BO-RYAKU (strategy)

Unconventional tactics of deception and battle, political plots, and advantageous timing for use of current events were used by Togakure ryu ninja. By employing or influencing seemingly outside forces to bring the enemy around to doing what the ninja wanted him to do, ninja were able to work their will without drawing undue attention to themselves.

15. CHO HO (espionage)

Methods of successful espionage were perfected. This included ways of locating and recruiting spies and served as a guide for using espionage agents most effectively.

16. INTON-JUTSU (escape and concealment)

Ninja were experienced masters in the ways of using nature to cover their exit, allowing them to "disappear" at will. The *goton-po* five elements of escape were based on a working familiarity with the creative use of earth, water, fire, metal, and wood aspects of nature and the environment.

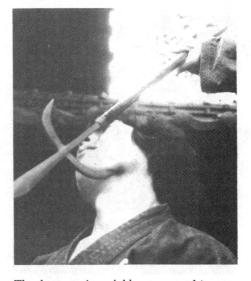

The *kamayari* or sickle spear used to snag an unsuspecting victim from above.

17. TEN-MON (meteorology)

Forecasting and taking advantage of weather and seasonal phenomena was an important part of any battle consideration. Ninja were trained to observe all the subtle signals from the environment in order to predict weather conditions.

18. CHI-MON (geography)

Knowing and successfully using the features of the terrain were crucial skills in the historical art of ninjutsu.

The weighted chain snakes out from the ninja's battlefield size *kusarigama*.

Though not listed as a separate item in the eighteen qualities above, a crucial part of the Togakure ryu ninja's training was the application of the *kyojitsu tenkan ho* philosophy. In the world of combat survival, the superior fighter makes use of all advantages at hand, including the influences of the mind. As a means of increasing the difficulty for an enemy, ninja of old developed the strategy of *kyojitsu tenkan ho*, or the interchange of the concepts of falsehood and actuality. A strategy for winning that relies on the presentation of truth and falsehood in ways that permit the antagonist to be deceived, *kyojitsu tenkan* forms the basic approach for all ninjutsu activities and thinking.

Because the ninja is dealing freely with the concepts of truth and falsehood, fluidly bending one into the other, he must be well grounded in his own concept of reality. To prevent becoming lost, misguided, or swallowed up by his own deception or awareness altering, the ninja must maintain *seishin*, or purity of heart. In this sense, the word *pure* means "complete" or "total." The ninja carries the truth in his heart, though he may appear in many psychological guises to others. His intentions remain resolute, though others may have no idea what those commitments entail. Because he is totally honest with himself at all levels of introspection, he can venture into the realm of falsehood and untruth without defiling himself or his spirit. He can willingly plunge into the cold darkness, knowing full well that he has the power to create his own light from the brightness he carries in his heart.

Togakure ryu ninja were skilled in the use of the *bisen-to* or broad-bladed halberd.

The historical ninja was a master of disguise and illusion as means of attaining his objectives. *Hensojutsu* impersonation skills were the first step towards learning to become invisible.

Kayakujutsu, the science of fire and explosives, demonstrated by Dr. Hatsumi with his handheld cannon.

Shinobi-iri stealth methods of ninjutsu were perfected as ways of entering the unenterable, and escaping the inescapable.

The *goton-po* of the ninja's *inton-jutsu* concealment method stressed the use of nature as an ally and tool for escape and evasion.

Submerged with a reed breathing tube, the ninja demonstrates one of the *sui-ren* water skills of ninjutsu.

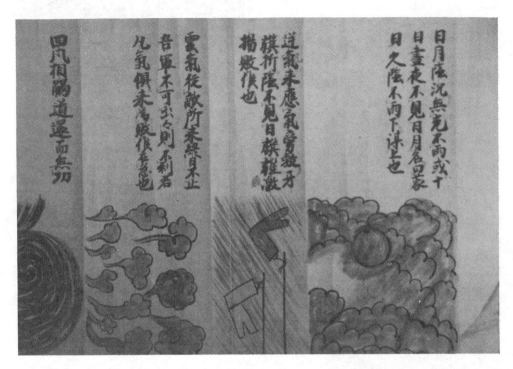

A hand-written scroll describing the *tenmon* meteorological conditions that could have an effect on battle plans.

TAIJUTSU UNARMED COMBAT

Taijutsu, literally translated as "skill with the body," forms the basis for all understanding in the fighting arts of ninjujutsu. By concentrating on developing natural responsive actions with the body during initial ninja training, one can then use the physical lessons as models for psychological and tactical training in advanced studies. The ninja's taijutsu is made up of methods for striking and grappling in unarmed fighting, tumbling and breaking falls, leaping and climbing, conditioning the body and maintaining health, as well as special ways of walking and running.

Some of the more popular Oriental martial arts and training systems attempt to mold the practitioners' ways of reacting and moving to fit a stylized set of predetermined movements. In effect, they are "adding to" the student's total personality. The taijutsu of Togakure ryu ninjutsu works in the opposite manner to naturalize all movements by stripping away the awkward or unnatural tendencies that may have been picked up unknowingly over the years.

As a fighting system, taijutsu relies on natural body strength and resiliency, speed of response and movement, and an understanding of the principles of nature, for successful results in self-protection. The techniques take advantage of natural physical construction and efficient employment of body dynamics. The students need not imitate some sort of animal, nor distort or deform the natural body structure, in order to employ the taijutsu techniques for self-defense.

The principles of taijutsu also provide the foundation for combat with weapons in ninjutsu. The loose, adaptive body postures and movements readily fit the fighting tools employed in the ninja's art. Footwork, body balance, speed, energy application, and strategy are identical for practicioners of ninjutsu, whether fighting with fists, blades, or chains.

The effectiveness of taijutsu as a total fighting system is based on the ninja's reliance on the harmony inherent in nature. Even the fundamental fighting postures and techniques model themselves after the manifestations of the elements in our environment, and advanced training methods use the balances of the psychological as well as the physical ways. The five elemental manifestations of the physical universe are the classifications of solid, liquid, combustious, gaseous, and sub-atomic potential, which are the *chi* (earth), *sui* (water), *ka* (fire), *fu* (wind), and *ku* (emptiness) of Oriental metaphysics. By increasing our observation and awareness of the inter-relationships of these various levels of reality, we can develop the ability to see vast patterns of cause and effect that are unrecognized by other people around us.

In this sense the practitioner of ninjutsu learns to use the natural progression of the universe to his benefit. His actions conform to the playing out of universal cycles, and his body and intentions always adapt to the advances of any attacker. By coming into attunement with the scheme of totality, the ninja always knows the appropriate response for any given situation that confronts him.

Junan taiso, the ninja's body conditioning method, contributes to the suppleness, speed, and responsiveness necessary for the effective application of taijutsu techniques. In Togakure Ryu ninjutsu training, strength is generated through flexibility. The muscles and joints are exercised to enhance their natural elastic qualities. The *junan taiso*, along with a proper diet, provides for strength, flexibility, and health, even through old age.

The muscular system can be developed in two distinct manners. Weak muscles can be built up and strengthened through vigorous repetitious exercise. This type of exercise is characterized by rapid contraction and relaxation of the muscles, and eventually produces a feeling of localized or general fatigue. In a different manner, tight or unresponsive muscles can be made more limber through relaxed stretching exercises. Popularized today by contemporary versions of Indian yoga, this type of conditioning is characterized by holding poses that stretch the muscles and joints for several seconds, while relaxing specific muscles and allowing them to extend to the natural limits for a healthy human body.

It should be stressed that the *junan taiso* conditioning exercises are of much greater significance than mere "warm-ups" for fighting practice in the training hall. The exercises actually form a basis for healthful living by presenting an opportunity to experience the mental and physical aspects of the body working in harmony. During the performance of the exercises, we observe the body tissues, fluid circulation, breathing patterns, and active direction of the consciousness, all in harmony with each other. By learning the effects and influences of the body's many maintenance systems, the student of ninjutsu can develop a working knowledge of his own power to control the health and condition of his body.

The head is just another part of the body, and we must learn to overcome the tendency to make a distinction between the brain and the other internal organs of the body. The body knows how to move if we let it, and it does not require active mental control to respond properly in a threatening situation. The student of ninjutsu works to eliminate the unwieldy process of first mechanically thinking through a response before actually carring it out. This naturalness of movement results from learning how all the functions work in coordination and balance with each other.

Taijutsu body skills, as illustrated in an ancient scroll depicting combat techniques perfected by ninja.

Stretching the leg muscles for limberness
and increasing the flexibility of the hip
joints are crucial for mobility, proper support of the body, and powerful leaps and
jumps.

Twisting and flexing the torso and neck increases suppleness and enhances the flow of energy through the spinal channel to the nerve pathways of the body trunk and limbs.

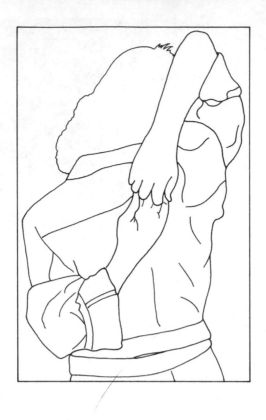

The arms and wrists are twisted to develop the flexibility necessary for overcoming adversaries, or escaping the restraining holds of others.

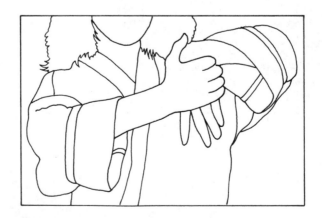

Kamae (Fighting Poses)

The body postures of taijutsu are more than mere utilitarian stances or formal ways of positioning the trunk and limbs. The *kamae* of ninjutsu can best be described as the physical embodiment of the mental outlook. In any living or fighting situation, the body and the consciousness it houses are constantly being subjected to the ever-progressing development of a series of present instants. In order to be the most effective in any of these given situations, the mind and body should be totally in tune with each other to prevent inappropriate actions or reactions. In actuality, "mind" and "body" are mere arbitrary terms that we apply to made-up divisions of one single entity.

When properly applied, the *kamae* reflects the ninja's heart. This means that our physical nature conforms naturally to our intentions, and there is no division between our interior and exterior aspects. This state of integrated mind and body action is totally natural, and can be observed readily in the movements of animals as they interact with their environment. Only human beings seem to develop the need to be trained in natural body motion.

The *kamae* themselves are mere guides or suggestions for the most effective use of the body weapon. As such, they are physical attitudes, and are by no means to be adhered to in precise imitation. Each individual body, with its unique configuration of muscles and bone alignments will naturally determine its own pragmatic and comfortable variations of the basic fighting postures. As the student progresses, the *kamae* become less and less significant as specific poses, as they are gradually assimilated into the character of the individual. Once these fundamentals are internalized, the most advanced fighting posture becomes a "no fighting posture."

34

Illustration of *kamae* fighting postures from an ancient Chinese scroll, showing the influence of Chinese boxing on the fighting methods of Japan's Togakure ryu ninjutsu tradition.

Observational Postures

The observational postures are used as the structural base from which the traditional greetings of respect, salutes, and bow proceed. In a culture that developed without the chairs of the western world, the observational postures provided a comfortable and yet dignified means to carry out conversation or personal interchange of ideas.

Gassho No Kamae

The *gassho* posture is the form for the standing salute or greeting. Both feet are firmly on the ground, and the hands are clasped in front of the chest with the elbows slightly elevated. The sight extends forward across the tops of the hands.

Fudoza No Kamae

The *fudoza* pose is a traditional Japanese seated posture. The left leg is folded beneath the body and the seat rests on the ankle of the left foot. The right leg is pulled in across the front with the sole of the right foot lodged against the left thigh. The back is straight, allowing the vertebrae of the spine to assume their natural positions in relation to each other. The gaze is leveled forward.

Seiza No Kamae

The *seiza* pose is a traditional Japanese kneeling posture. The legs are folded beneath the body and the seat rests on the heels of both feet. The body trunk is straight with the knees slightly separated and the hands resting on the thighs. The bow of respect proceeds from the kneeling position by extending the hands forward onto the floor and lowering the forehead forward.

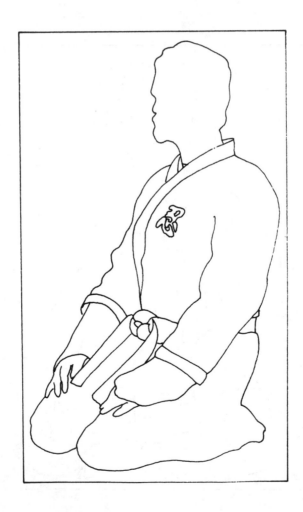

Defensive Fighting Postures

The defensive postures are used when reacting to attacks with blocks or avoidances before executing counter techniques. The body shifts or slides angularly to cut inside or outside of the attack, and blocks are applied with injurious force from the safe distance created.

Ichimonji No Kamae

The *ichimonji* pose is assumed as the body slides back and away from the attack. The rear leg carries most of the weight and the leading leg holds the body upright. The shoulders are relaxed and low, and the open hands protect the face and body or intercept the attacker's advance.

Doko No Kamae

The *doko* pose is assumed as the body leaps or shifts away from the attack. The rear leg carries most of the weight and the lead leg provides the springing motion to push the body back. The leading hand intercepts or blocks the attacker's advance and the rear hand is held in preparation for a counter blow.

Hicho No Kamae

The *hicho* pose clears the leading leg from sweeping or toppling attacks, and hold the leg in preparation for defensive kicking as the adversary approaches. The balance is maintained by slightly flexing the ground leg knee, and the arms are held in protective positions from which they can grab, block, or deliver strikes.

Receiving Fighting Postures

The receiving postures are used when responding to attacks with techniques that harmonize or go with the adversary's power and delivery. The body pivots or moves laterally to blend with the attacker's motion, and protective counter attacks are delivered simultaneously.

Shizen No Kamae

The *shizen* pose is the natural standing posture of the human body. The mind is alert, and the body is relaxed and ready to move and adapt to any situation. Each foot supports an equal amount of body weight, and the shoulders are relaxed with the arms hanging naturally at the sides. The natural posture of the body position from which most surprise attacks, self-defense action will develop, as it resembles everyday standing or walking poses.

Hira Ichimonji No Kamae

The *hira ichimonji* pose is a balanced standing position from which the body can shift or pivot in reaction to an attacker's advances. Each foot supports an equal amount of weight, and the shoulders are relaxed with both arms extended horizontally at the sides. The arms can be used to sweep, grab, or deliver strikes as the body adapts to the attacker's motion.

Hoko No Kamae

The *hoko* pose is another adaptive fighting position from which the body can respond to an attack. The weight is equally distributed over both feet, and the arms are held above the shoulders in a slightly bowed position. The arms can be used to trap, deflect, or deliver strikes as the body hops or shifts with the attack.

Attacking Fighting Postures

Jumonji No Kamae

The *jumonji* pose is characterized by the crossed-wrist hand position, which protects the body during advancing attacks. The elbows cover the rib cage, and the fists cover the neck and face areas before delivering striking techniques. The body weight is maintained with a slightly forward balance, and the footwork pushes the body solidly in the attacking direction.

Kosei No Kamae

The *kosei* pose is used to deliver attacking movements while allowing for the interception of possible counter attacks from the adversary. The leading hand is used to grab, deflect, or divert the adversary's attention while the rear hand carries out the attacking technique.

The *kihon kata*, or fundamental practice guides, of ninjutsu unarmed fighting are the first steps toward mastery of the use of mind and body as a total entity. The techniques are initially practiced with the consciousness directed towards understanding the purpose and practical application of the physical movements. Next, the student begins to work on making the technique a natural part of his knowledge; in effect, allowing his body to develop the natural ability to perform the technique. Finally, the technique itself is dropped from consciousness as a technique, and becomes yet one more variation of the body and personality to handle things in an effective manner.

The specific techniques themselves number in the thousands, and include countless variations. The students are not expected to memorize the movements of each technique, but rather work on internalizing the principles embodied by the techniques. The vast amount of memorization would distract the student from concentrating on and acknowledging his current abilities. His training would involve too much emphasis on "becoming" skilled in the future instead of "being" skilled, to the fullest degree possible, in the present. Extensive memorization of external forms of movement also reduces the student's familiarity with natural spontaneous action, hindering development of mind and body integration. This spontaneity, or automatically responding with the appropriate reaction to the elements of the circumstances, is a crucial skill for successful self-protection. The ninja is prepared to adapt to any situation that confronts him, and is not tempted to force the situation to fit the parameters of some specialized training system.

The fundamental techniques can be classified in three broad categories of action. *Taihenjutsu* includes all methods of individual body movement; the breakfalls, rolls, leaps, and walking methods unique to ninjutsu. *Dakentaijutsu* includes the strikes, kicks, and punches, as well as blocking techniques of the ninja unarmed fighting system. *Jutaijutsu* is the grappling method for throwing, choking, locking, and escaping the restraining holds of others. Actual self-protection, whether fighting an animal or another human being or surviving a fall from a moving vehicle, is always a string of instants in which we relate our body and consciousness to external forces. The broad scope of ninjutsu training has therefore evolved to include methods to handle anything. The man who is only trained to punch will encounter greater difficulty in situations where his punching skills are ineffective or inappropriate. The grappling expert will be frustrated by the adversary who stays outside his reach and strikes at his grabbing limbs. True proficiency in self-protection comes from a blending of all areas of skill with the body, and cannot result from the dangerous and limiting concept of "developing a speciality."

Ukemi (Breakfalls)

The *ukemi*, or ground hitting techniques of ninjutsu are practiced extensively in the early stages of training, in order to familiarize the student with the adaptive nature of his body, and cultivate a natural suppleness and elasticity. The rolling and handspring breakfalls are used to accommodate situations in which the ninja is forced to the ground, whether thrown, knocked down, or tripped by an assailant or natural elements in the environment. A feeling of non-resistance, acceptance of the circumstances, and determination to use the circumstances to our advantage, is permitted to guide both the mind and body for successful self-protection.

The basic fundamental techniques of the ninja's *taihenjutsu ukemi* include the following methods of body movement that allow the ninja to move or hit the ground in a manner that permits him to accommodate the attack safely.

Rolling methods, in which the body curls towards the ground surface to take the ninja away from danger
Forward roll
Right roll
Left roll
Backward roll
Handspring methods, in which the body vaults away from danger or extended arms that are braced against the ground surface
Forward handspring
Right handspring
Left handspring
Body drop methods, in which the body drops straight to the ground surface to move away from danger.
Forward breakfall
Right body drop
Rear body drop
Leaping methods, in which the feet propel the body away from danger while the body remains in an upright position
Forward leap
Left leap
Backward leap
High jump
Downward jump.

Zenpo Kaiten (Forward Roll)

The leading arm and shoulder are lowered to the ground as the body curls forward into the roll. The body stays tucked so that the ninja can roll right up into position to continue the fight. In the example ninjutsu master-instructor Tsunehisa Tanemura completes the forward roll and is prepared to continue with a shuriken throwing star which he pulls from a concealed pocket in his jacket.

Soku Ho Kaiten (Sideways Roll)

The arm and shoulder are lowered to the side as the body curls and topples toward the ground. The ninja keeps his body curled so that he can roll right up onto his feet again to continue the fight. In the example, grandmaster Dr. Hatsumi dives out to his left to avoid a downward slash from a war sword in front of him. As he regains his footing at the completion of the roll, Dr. Hatsumi executes a lunging fist strike that propels his attacker on over his back with the initial motion generated from the sword strike itself.

Soku Ho Tobi (Sideways leap)

The hips are slammed in the direction of travel, and the trailing foot pushes off to give the body additional momentum. The sideways leaps, as are the forward and backward leaps, are lateral shifts of the body's position. They are not bounding jumps in which the ninja springs up and crashes down. The hips remain fairly level throughout the entire side-shifting action. In this example, ninjutsu master-instructor Fumio Manaka performs a sideways leap, taking him across a level grassy expanse.

Tobi Keri (Leaping with a kick)

The feet and legs send the body straight up and forward with a simultaneous kicking action against the adversary. The body remains compacted to reduce the effective target areas for the adversary's counter-kicks.

Body Weapons

The martial skill of taijutsu is a generalized total body method of dealing with situations that demand response. As such, it is not a specialized system or art form restricted to punches, throws, or holds alone. The total body is used as the defensive weapon. In ninjutsu training, we use the word *ken* to describe all natural body weapons, though the term is usually limited to the standard clenched fist in most of the other martial arts systems that employ punching techniques. This broad interpretation of the word better fits the attitude of flexibility that guides ninja taijutsu training.

Just as the body posture is constantly changing, adjusting, and adapting to new spatial and psychological conditions, the body weapons are also constantly in a state of change and adaptation. Grabbing hands turn into punching fists which become pinching or tearing claws, and sweeping feet suddenly lift to deliver kicks or propel knee slams. Shoulders used for arm leverage drop into position as ramming tools, and hips are transformed from body carriers to slamming weapons.

Another characteristic of the ninjutsu fighting method is the use of natural body dynamics for power behind the weapons. Rather than tensing the muscles and violently shifting the skeletal structure to generate strong strikes, the ninja's taijutsu utilizes the unification of the body's energy, balanced structure, and breath timing to create knock-down power. The whole body delivers the technique, rather than a limited portion such as the arm or lower half of the leg. This natural power and delivery speed is sufficient when combined with a scientific application against strategic weak points of the body.

Kikaku Ken (Head Strike)

The bone structure of the head is used to slam, butt, or ram bone targets on the assailant's body, and can also be used to exert leverage against the joints of the limbs. When grabbed from behind, the head can be rocked back to exert painful pressure against the attacker's face. While applying a series of low uppercut punches to an assailant's midsection, the chin can be dropped to lower the forehead into position for slamming the face or chest.

Kikaku ken used for head butting.

Kikaku ken used against the attacker's swinging arm.

Shuki Ken (Elbow strike)

The bone structure of the elbow is used to strike the bones in the limbs, torso, and head of the attacker, and can be used to apply crushing pressure to sensitive points of the body. Using the movement of the entire body for power, the elbow is used to deliver damaging strikes within ranges too close for punches.

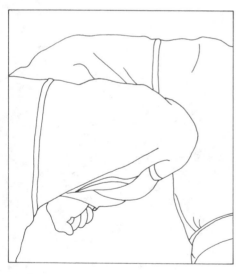

Shuki ken elbow strike.

Shuki ken used for leverage against the attacker's shoulder joint.

Sokki Ken (Knee strike)

The bone points of the knee are used to strike the bones in the limbs, torso, and head of the assailant, and can also be used to apply crushing pressure to weaker points of the body. The knee rises, drops, or rams into its target within ranges and angles too awkward for punches and kicks.

Sokki ken knee slamming strike.

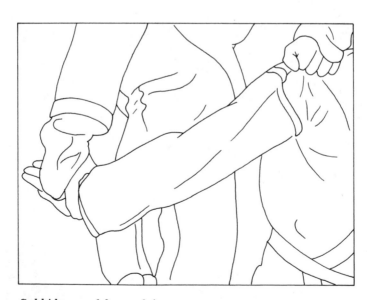

Sokki ken used for applying pressure.

Shito Ken (Thumb strike)

The tip of the thumb is used for driving jabs into the semi-soft targets of the assailant's body, and for exerting pressure against sensitive points of the body. The muscular system is particularly vulnerable to pressure point attacks, especially in areas where the muscles cover the bones, such as the insides of the thigh or upper arm, the rib cage, and the sides of the neck. The fingers curl beneath the protruding thumb for support.

Shito ken extended knuckle fist.

Shito ken in action.

Shishin Ken ("Finger needle" strike)

The *shishin ken* "finger needle" is used for executing short close-range stabs to soft and semi-soft targets such as the face, neck, solar plexus, and underarms.

Shishin ken finger needle.

Shishin ken used against the adversary's throat to force him to the ground with a neck twist.

Shitan Ken (Thumb pressure strike)

The thumbs, as well as the middle and pointer fingers, are used as hooks to snag, tear, grip, or apply pressure to sensitive areas of the body. The bone structure of the digits provides the pressure, and the nails can also be used to create additional pain for more leverage when subduing an attacker.

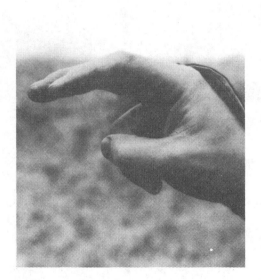

Shitan ken finger hooks.

Shitan ken used to lift and sling an attacker to the ground.

Shitan ken used to apply crushing pressure against the assailant's hand and wrist.

Hooking the sensitive tissues of an attacker's face to stop his throwing action.

Kiten Ken (Shuto open hand strike)

The outer edge of the open hand is used to attack the bones of the arms, legs, neck, and head. The strike is applied at a 90° angle, perpendicular to the target area, and is slammed completely through the space taken up by the target. The entire body motion is used to provide power, and rather than flicking into place and back, the open hand strike should knock the adversary completely off balance.

Kiten ken.

Kiten ken used against the attacker's trapped leg.

Shikan Ken (Extended knuckle fist)

The extended knuckles are used to strike broad areas of the bone on the assailant's body, such as the lower portion of the rib cage, the breastbone, and the face. The fingers are half-folded, and the elongated fist uses the bone points of the middle knuckles to apply damaging punches that knock the adversary back. The entire body delivers the power, and the hand flexes open right before impact, shooting the knuckles forward.

Shikan ken extended knuckle fist.

The *kiten ken* or *shuto* hand edge and the *shikanken* extended knuckle fist can be seen as applied in the unarmed technique series known as *Koku*, or "Tiger sky." The attacker moves in with a right lunging punch. In the photos, Dr. Hatsumi counters with a stopping strike using his left fist against the inside of the attacker's punching arm. Immediately he slams the edge of his open right hand into the bone of the attacker's forearm. The attacker then attempts a groin kick as his stunned arm is knocked away. Dr. Hatsumi leaps to the outside of the kicking leg and simultaneously counters with a rising shin kick of his own. He then throws his kicking leg forward and uses his body weight in motion to propel a right *shikan ken* punch into the attacker's right lower ribs.

Shako Ken (Claw strike)

With the fingers spread and slightly curled, the hand can form a claw weapon for use against the soft areas of the assailant's body. The palm portion slams or crushes and the fingers rake or drive. The face, throat, abdomen, groin, and muscles of the upper chest along the inside of the thigh are all effective targets for the hand claw.

Shako ken.

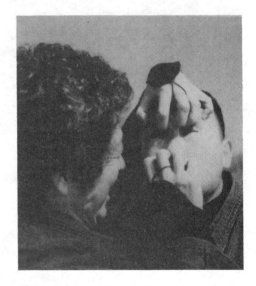

Shako ken used for ripping technique.

The *shako ken* or clawing hand can be used in grappling applications as well as striking techniques, or the two methods can be combined to handle the same attack. The attacker reaches forward and grabs Dr. Hatsumi by the jacket lapel, intending to sling him to the ground with a throw. Dr. Hatsumi counters by dropping his body weight slightly and covering the attacker's hand with his own. Using the palm of his right hand in a *shako ken* position, Dr. Hatsumi shoves the attacker's thumb back towards his wrist with a crushing sliding motion. As the attacker's thumb joints fold in against themselves and he attempts to withdraw away from the pain, Dr. Hatsumi steps forward with a *shako ken* clawing smash to the attacker's windpipe, lifting him up and then slamming him down on his back.

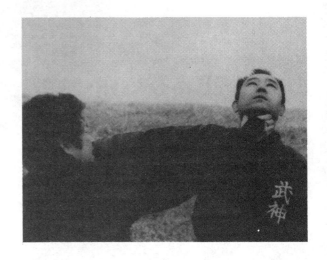

Fudo Ken ("Immovable" or clenched fist)

The clenched fist is used for strikes and punches applied to the edges of the bone structure in the assailant's body. The *fudo ken* can be delivered effectively from a variety of angles, using the front or back of the primary knuckles, the bottom edges of the middle knuckles, or the base of the fist along the outer edge, to break bone targets and knock the attacker to the ground.

Fudo ken.

Fudo ken used against the forearm of a sword-wielding attacker.

Soku Yaku (Foot strike)

The bottom surface of the foot is used to ram or crush the semi-soft or hard targets on the assailant's body. The kick is propelled into its target with a lateral or descending stomping motion, and utilizes the ball or heel portion of the sole of the foot. The kick drives through the target with knock-down force, and does not slap the target and pull back quickly.

Soku yaku used in a *zenpo geri* forward kick.

Soku yaku used as a *sokuho geri* sideways kick.

Soku yaku used as a *koho geri* backward kick.

Tobi keri jumping kick using the *soku yaku* foot sole weapon.

The *fudo ken* or clenched fist and the *soku yaku* sole of the foot can be seen as applied in an unarmed defense against a knife slashing attack. The attacker moves in with a right downward slashing cut. Dr. Hatsumi counters by leaping foward with a left *fudo ken* punch at the attacker's face, using his left elbow to fend off the attacker's right arm if necessary. After completing the punch, he continues to grind the knuckles of his left fist into the attacker's face in order to control the attacker's movement while he uses his right hand to grab the attacker's neck and shoulder assembly. Still controlling the attacker's right knife arm, Dr. Hatsumi leaps up onto the attacker's body with a rib-crushing leg lock. He then lowers his back to the ground and secures a firm hold on the attacker's ankles and heels. Using his hips for leverage, Dr. Hatsumi then pulls out the attacker's legs, slamming him onto the ground backwards. A *soku yaku* heel stamp from beneath the chin knocks the attacker unconscious as it breaks his neck.

Soku Gyaku (Toe strike)

The tips of the extended toes are used for stabbing or driving kicks into soft or semi-soft body targets such as the abdomen, neck, and muscles along the insides of the arms and legs. The kick is propelled into its target with a swing-ing or plunging motion, with the toes clenched together to rein-force each other. The kick can be used to ram through the target, or merely to cause enough pain to distract the assailant.

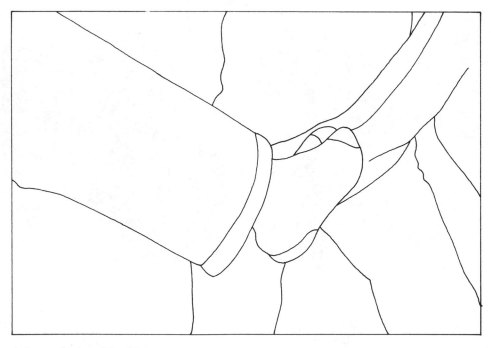

Soku gyaku toe drive kick.

In this technique, Dr. Hatsumi uses the *soku gyaku* toe drive kick against the attacker's lower abdomen in order to lift him up and back with the momentum of the moving foot. Just as the kick reaches its full extension, Dr. Hatsumi pulls his right leg back with a wide swinging motion to his right. The kicking foot hits across the assailant's left hip bone and sends him flying to his left as Dr. Hatsumi drops his right foot back into position behind his left foot in preparation for a possible follow-up technique if it is necessary.

Shizen Ken ("Natural" or body weapon)

The *shizen ken* "natural weapon" and the *tai ken* "total body weapon" include countless variations of the body parts used as weapons for defense. In addition to the various named techniques, the shoulders, back of the wrist, fingernails, shins, teeth, indeed whatever works and is in position, are used to subdue the attacker intent on harming or killing us.

Fingernails raking down on the tender skin of the scalp and ear structure.

Knees, hands and elbows used to smash an assailant into the ground.

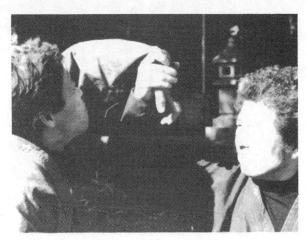

Using the back of the wrist to lift an attacker's arm.

Using the shoulder to jam the kick of an attacker.

Using the body weight to crush an attacker.

The *Shizen ken* principle applied by using the forearm to choke or block the kicking action of an attacker.

Dakentaijutsu Conditioning the Weapons

The ninja's *dakentaijutsu* striking techniques combine the methods of two distinct disciplines that are said to have originally developed in China. *Koppojutsu* bone smashing strikes utilize the heavier or more solid bones of the ninja's body as weapons. The *koppo* techniques use the clenched fists, bottoms of the feet, knees, and elbows, to attack and break up the bone structure of the adversary. *Koshijutsu* organ and muscle stabbing strikes utilize the tips of the extended fingers and toes as weapons against the softer internal targets of the aversary.

A series of four progressive developmental steps can be followed when first pursuing the skills of effective striking, whether with the upper or lower extremities.

1. Learn and internalize the proper feeling when applying each of the body's weapons. Isolate the hand or foot that is doing the striking and concentrate on the delivery of strike alone. Weapon accuracy is the key to this first step.

2. Once proper command of the weapon itself is developed, work on the additional elements of utilizing all the possible footwork variations and body angles that could propel the weapon into its target. Proper distancing is the key to this second step, as the entire body comes into play.

3. Use an appropriate striking target for actual application of the strike. The purpose of a strike is to stun or knock down an assailant, and the only way to develop a consistantly reliable strike is to work at actually striking a target over and over again repetitively. The key skill for development in this third stage is the ability to regulate and direct the impact of the weapon against the target.

4. Once sufficient technical skill in using the weapon has been developed, the fourth step is to utilize the energy and movement of the entire body when applying the strike. Far more effective than merely flexing the muscles and moving the bones of the striking limb alone, the ninja's taijutsu engages the motion of the entire body to generate the power of the strike. By combining the natural release of the breath with the expansive movement of the body from a base at the natural center of gravity, power is a product of the entire body in relaxed yet vibrant motion. The key to the effectiveness of the fourth step is the creation of thrust as a result of natural resilient motion rather than as a result of tension.

Ninjutsu master instructor Tetsuji Ishi-zuka uses the *shikan ken* punch against a padded striking target.

Ninjutsu instructor Shidoshi Stephen Hayes drills the *soku yaku* foot stamp against a tree trunk target.

Ninjutsu master intructor Tsunehisa Tanemura works at conditioning his hands on a rock surface, applying the *shako ken* clawing strike.

Ninjutsu instructor Shidoshi Kobayashi executes *kikaku ken* head butting strikes against a rock target.

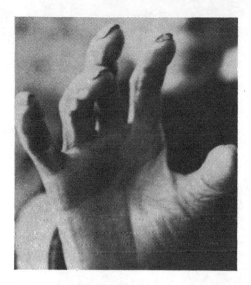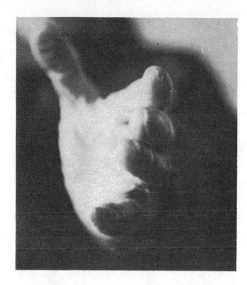

The toughened hands and feet of Togakure ryu 33rd grandmaster Toshitsugu Takamatsu show the results of conditioning after decades of *koshijutsu* striking training. Grandmaster Takamatsu could easily strip the bark from the trunks of trees with what appeared to observers to be effortless passes of his deadly hands.

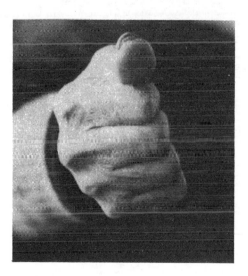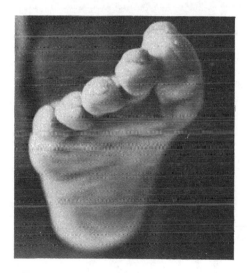

FIGHTING TOOLS OF NINJUTSU

According to the writings passed down from generation to generation in the Togakure ryu, the ninja's role in the playing out of history is primarily one of quiet, undetected influence that leads what appear to be random, unrelated incidents into coordination, balance, and harmony with the scheme of totality. In simpler terms, the ninja's job is to subtlely, stealthfully "encourage" things to be the way they are supposed to be.

In a handwritten *densho* scroll explaining the purpose of ninjutsu, my teacher, Toshitsugu Takamatsu lists the duties, responsibilities, and priorities for the Togakure ryu ninja agents of past generations.

1. Stealthy reconnaissance is the ninja's chief contribution to victory. The ninja should move undetected into the enemy's area of influence and gather pertinent information about the enemy's strengths and weaknesses. Escaping in a manner that prevents his presence from ever being known, the ninja then returns to his allies with the knowledge that will permit an attack at the most opportune time and place, leaving the enemy bewildered by the fact that the attack "just happened" to befall them at their weakest point.

2. Universal justice and a peaceful balance in society are the ninja's motivations. The ninja does not use his advanced skills and powers for mere self-protection or greed-inspired profit. Family, community, homeland, and "appropriateness" determine when a ninja should act, not power, money, political obligation, or thrill of violence and adventure.

3. The ninja relies on the power of universal laws to fulfill his intentions. Using a working knowledge of the *kyojitsu tenkan* theory of alternating appearances of reality, the ninja accomplishes his mission by concealing his own influence on the situation and preserving the impression that all is going according to fate alone. If the ninja is by chance detected, he will use everything and anything available in order to preserve and continue the usefulness of his mission.

4. The ninja works to accomplish his goals by having others unknowingly act out his wishes for him. Illusion, manipulative reverse psychology, fire and explosives as distractions, unique ninja equipment, chemicals and drugs, and even the plants and animals of nature are all tools in the ninja's behind-the-scenes direction of the events that will later be known as history. Only in the rarest of extreme cases does the ninja actually expose his influence by taking direct action and killing someone.

In reviewing Takamatsu Sensei's observations on the teachings of the Toda family grandmasters of Togakure ryu, it quickly becomes apparent that the tales portraying ninja as cold-hearted criminally-minded professional murders are grossly exaggerating the true story of Japan's history. Certainly, previous centuries in Japan did have their share of assassin, thieves, and saboteurs who imitated the physical ways of the ninja and would perform any task for the right amount of money. Without moral and spiritual guidance from the head of a major ninjutsu ryu or clan, however, these desperate persons were not even shadows of the true ninja of Japan, and therefore do not concern us at all.

Because the ninja's primary role as an advisor, scout, and consultant to the contending forces of the period, skills of espionage, psychological evaluation, and occult "sixth-sense" powers took precedence over battlefield combat skills. Though the historical ninja were well-known as accomplished and relentless fighters, the nature of their work was usually such that if they did have to engage in self-protection combat, it meant that their mission was automatically reduced in effectiveness due to their detection. For this reason, the ninja's weapons were usually considered as back up measures in case of failure, and not as the primary means of effectiveness as would be the case with the samurai warrior of old.

As a general rule, the fighting tools of ninjutsu usually incorporated the qualities of compactness, multiple usage (serving more than one purpose), and potential for deceptive application. Unlike the beautifully crafted weapons of the samurai, the ninja's tools were most often utilitarian implements turned out by an underground shop. Durability and ruggedness were their outstanding qualities, and aesthetic considerations usually lost out to pragmatism and economy.

The technique applications using ninjutsu fighting tools employ the same footwork, body dynamics, and energy concepts that are taught in the ninja's *taijutsu* unarmed fighting system. The purpose is to bring the enemy down as quickly as possible. The body weight in motion supplies the power for the weapon strikes, which have a slamming effect when applied, rather than a stinging effect.

Ninja ken or shinobigatana (Ninja Sword)

The *ninja ken*, sometimes referred to as *shinobigatana*, or short sword was an important tool in Japan's historical art of ninjutsu. However, when compared with the beautiful *tachi* and *katana* blades of the samurai, which were often masterpieces of swordmaking art, the ninja sword appears to be little more than a utilitarian bush knife. The ninja looked upon his sword as one of many tools of his trade, and though he respected its capabilities and value to his work, the ninja rarely afforded his short sword the reverence or spiritual qualities with which the samurai would regard his family treasure blade.

Ninja swords were much shorter than the samurai blades, in order to facilitate fighting in close quarters and moving quickly and silently down narrow corridors and crawl spaces. The blades were often straight slabs of steel with a single ground edge, because many ninja either had no access to or could not afford the work of expert swordmakers, and resorted to forging their own blades in home shops. The important *tsuba* handguard, often a delicate and prized work of art on samurai family swords, was also most often "home made" on *ninja ken*, and usually took the form of a hammered steel square without ornamentation. The ninja sword's scabbard was often longer in length than the blade itself, the extra space in the bottom end of the *saya* or sheath being used to carry messages, blinding powders, or explosives.

The historical ninja did in fact regard his short sword as more of a tool than an exclusive-use killing weapon. The blade was often used as a means of cutting through or prying open doors, hatches, or window frames. The extra-long *sageo* or scabbard cord could be used to bind captured enemies, rig up trip wires in front of doorways or along forest paths, or form a web seat for observation high up in the branches of a tree. The wide *tsuba* or hand guard could be used as a prying device, or by leaning the sword up against a wall, as a booster step for climbing.

Because the *ninja ken* was usually not as long nor as refined a blade as that of the samurai warrior, the method of using the ninja sword was different from that of conventional Japanese *kenjutsu*. The samurai could rely on the razor edge of his sword to make effective cuts, and he could thereby employ precise, sharp, graceful body movements to propel his sword. The ninja, on the other hand, had to rely more on body weight in motion behind the sword, in order to cut effectively. The less refined edge on his blade made the ninja's sword fighting techniques rely more on slamming stabs and sawing dragged-edge cuts, than the deft slashes that could be applied with the samurai sword.

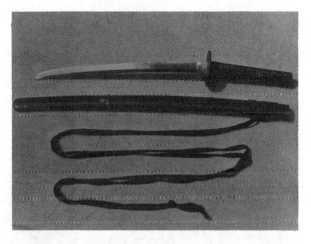

Ninja ken short sword of ninjutsu.

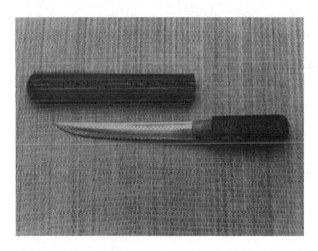

Shinobi tanto concealed short bladed fighting knife carried by ninja.

Mythical *tengu*, half crow and half human, engage in sword combat. The *tengu* were said to be the legendary forerunners of Japan's ninja, and the stories of the superstitious tell of the *tengu's* ability to know and effect the outcome of the future.

A ninja waits in a tree above a roadway, with sword poised for a falling stab at the enemy as he passes by below.

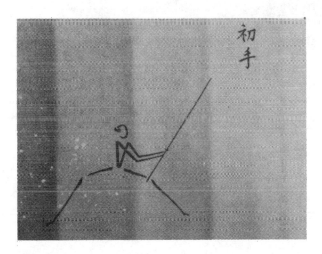

Illustration from a scroll showing the techniques of swordsmanship.

Dr. Masaaki Hatsumi crouches to his right to avoid a sword thrust attack from the front. As he moves forward and right, he simultaneously executes a horizontal sword slash across the lower portion of the attacker's leading knee. The grandmaster then quickly captures the attacker's sword with his left hand, and uses an upward slicing pull with the sword in his right hand to remove the sword from the attacker's grip. The technique leaves the attacker unarmed and at the mercy of the one originally attacked.

The ninja sword fighting method is a total body endeavor. In this example, the grandmaster uses his left arm to deflect the attacker's moving arms and knock the sword off its course. He then pulls back on the attacker's hair with his left hand while using his right hand and his body torso to pressure the sword edge into his adversary's midsection.

Dr. Hatsumi demonstrates that it is the body in motion, and not the limbs alone, that propels the blade for effective cutting. Even when used at extremely close ranges, the ninja method of using the body behind the blade is the key to devastating sword work.

Shidoshi Stephen Hayes, a grand-master Masaaki Hatsumi's sole American disciple and head of Togakure ryu training in the United States, shows one of the ninja's *iai* sword drawing techniques. The sword is drawn from the scabbard edge up. The elbow rises up and then moves forward and down to bring the sword edge across the target with a downward diagonal cut.

The actual blade of the *ninja ken* was often much shorter than the scabbard in which it was carried, which allowed room for blinding powders that could be used to star-tle an enemy in combat. The cut-away photo shows the hollow end of the ninja *saya* and its powdered contents.

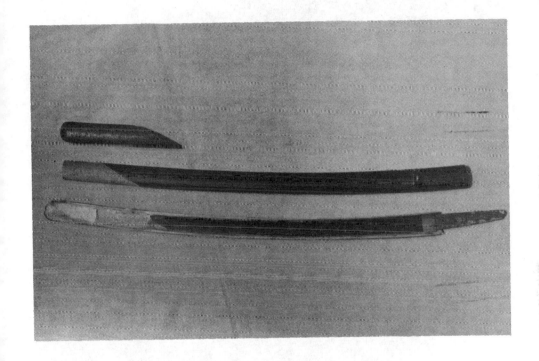

Grandmaster Masaaki Hatsumi demonstrates the use of the *ninja ken* scabbard as a tool for blasting a load of blinding powder into the face of a sword-bearing adversary.

Shinobi-zue (Ninja Staffs and Canes)

Historically, sticks, staffs, and canes have always been staple weapons in the Japanese culture, for commoners and samurai alike. It was only natural that the ninja would adopt the fighting staff as one of their standard tools as well. Readily available, unobtrusive, and easily mastered as a weapon, sticks and staffs are still just as important for students of ninjutsu today.

Shinobi-zue, ninja canes, vary in length from three to six or seven feet. In many cases, the ninja's cane or walking staff also contained a variety of hidden weapons. Ninjutsu *shikomi-zue* were hollowed out to conceal blades, chains, hooks, arrows, climbing aids, and even poison liquids or gasses. Other canes could be transformed into underwater breathing tubes or silent blowguns.

The weapon familiarization process is a crucial first step towards building up competence with the fighting staff, just as it is with natural body weapons and other external tools.

Here, Dr. Hatsumi demonstrates a deflecting high block and counter-strike to trip the attacker.

In the two-photo sequence that follows, the technique is shown applied to an armed attacker.

Application 1

Application 2

Body weight in motion behind the strike generates the power in the Togakure ryu stick fighting method. The arms alone are not merely swung around into the target. In the clash sequence shown here, a sword-bearing assailant leaps back and away from Masaaki Hatsumi's low-level slam to the knees. As the attacker begins his attempt at countering, Dr. Hatsumi lunges forward with his left leg, using his advancing body weight behind the staff to knock the attacker's arms and blade back. The grandmaster again lunges forward, this time on his right leg, and slams his staff into the kidney region of his assailant to subdue him.

Armed with the cane-length *hanbo*, the grandmaster drops into a crouch and slips inside the attacker's arm in response to an attempted strike. As he moves, Masaaki Hatsumi slams the tip edge of his cane into the forward-moving ribs of his attacker. He then secures the assailant's right attacking wrist and exerts leverage from beneath the attacker's right shoulder joint. Shifting his weight forward onto his left leg, the grandmaster uses his cane to knock the attacker backwards. Once on the ground, the attacker is held in place by the cane, which extends painfully from beneath his right ribs across the inside of his right arm and is held in position by crushing pressure from Dr. Hatsumi's left knee. The grandmaster applies a final stunning blow from close range with his left fist.

111

In this application of *han-bojutsu* defensive stick fighting, the grandmaster grips his cane in the standard walking-stick fashion. He lunges forward with a lateral swinging strike to the ribs, jamming the attacker's attempt to strike. Dr. Hatsumi then moves to the attacker's right side, away from a possible strike from the left fist. He controls the attacker's right arm with his shoulder and chin. Rolling his right fist into position under the cane and grabbing the free end with his left hand, Dr. Hatsumi next snaps inward with crushing pressure against the attacker's rib cage beneath his left arm. The grandmaster then spins to his left while dropping his hips, and throws his trapped assailant onto the ground.

Dr. Hatsumi steps to the outside of an attacker's kick, and swings the end of his cane up into the bottom of the attacker's calf. He then uses his right elbow to exert trapping pressure against the attacker's right ankle while using his stick to apply inward pressure on the inside of the attacker's right shin. With a twist of his shoulders and hips, Dr. Hatsumi then topples his assailant to the ground, where he continues to hold the trapped right leg as a means of controlling the attacker's movement.

Dr. Hatsumi shifts forward and to the outside of the attacker's right arm, in response to an attempted lunge punch. He cracks the end of his cane down against the bones of the attacker's right wrist to deflect the strike. The grandmaster then shoves his cane forward, over the top of the attacker's stunned wrist, and passes it beneath the attacker's right upper arm to force the arm to bend. Dr. Hatsumi then pulls up while pushing forward, applying pressure on the attacker's shoulder joint. As the attacker tenses up to prevent his shoulder from being torn apart, he is forced forward on his face on the ground. Dr. Hatsumi then uses his left knee to immobilize the attacker while jamming the tip of his cane into the right side of the attacker's neck to subdue him.

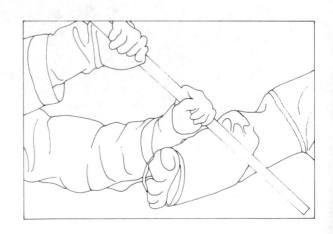

Even routine non-weapon tools can be pressed into service with the techniques of ninjutsu's *bojutsu* stick and staff fighting. Here the *daisharin* wheel and axle assembly is used as a combat staff to knock the legs out from beneath an attacker.

A *Shingon* priest's *suzu-zue* ring-topped walking staff is used as a fighting staff to subdue a sword-wielding attacker. The grandmaster does not bother to block the incoming slash. Instead, he uses a direct stabbing attack to the assailant's face to stun him, and then quickly grabs the immobilized weapon to end the clash.

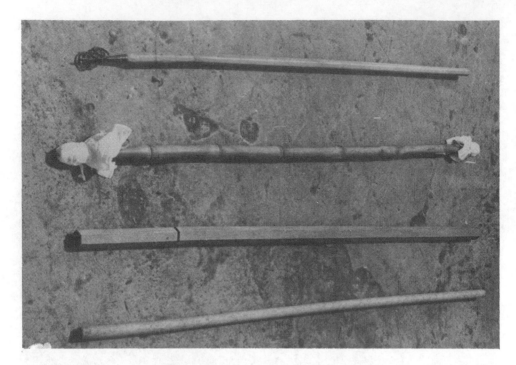

Ninja canes with their hidden weapons.

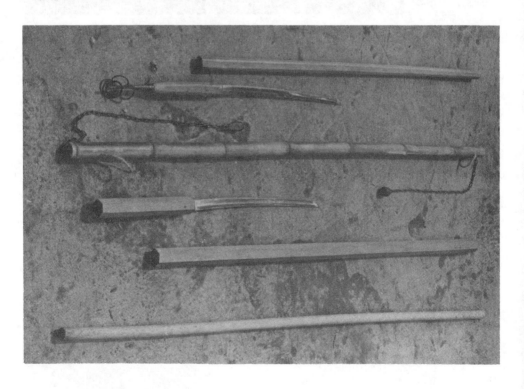

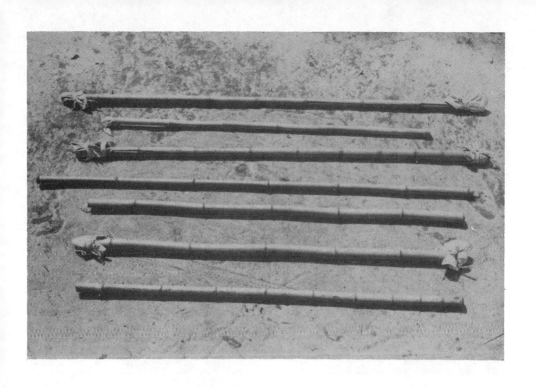

A hidden spear point leaps out from the end of the grandmaster's staff in response to his attacker's charge.

A ninja chained battlefield staff snares the enemy and controls his position for the application of further techniques.

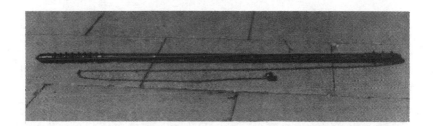

As an assailant moves forward with upraised sword, Dr. Hatsumi swings the upper end of his *shikomi-zue* down at the legs of his attacker. The concealed chain rattles out and its hooked end snags the attacker's leading leg. Using his body weight in motion to generate power, the grandmaster rocks back to pull the chain taut and topple his assailant.

Tessen (Iron War Fan)

The *tessen* iron war fan was often used in applications that were similar to those in which a short stick, club, or truncheon was employed. The war fan could be constructed from a single slab of iron, in which case it merely resembled a folded fan without being able to serve as a true fan. The solid fans were designed solely as weapons and signs of authority. The *tessen* could also be constructed of iron ribs with heavy paper or silk folds that formed a true fan while retaining the heft and strength of a clubbing weapon for defensive purposes.

In the following technique, Dr. Hatsumi jams his *tessen* iron fan into the base of his attacker's blade as it descends. Note that he hits just above the attacker's hand in order to reduce the attacker's effective strike leverage. The grandmaster next deflects the blade to his right (the adversary's left) and slips around to the attacker's right side while gaining control of his blade. Dr. Hatsumi pulls the fan against the inside of the attacker's right wrist while shoving forward against the attacker's right elbow in order to immobilize the sword. The grandmaster then continues on around the attacker's right side into position behind him and subdues his adversary with repeated stabbing strikes using the end of his *tessen* against the lower ribs and kidneys.

127

Shuko and Ashiko (Spiked Hand and Foot Bands)

Two specialty tool/weapons of the historical Togakure ryu ninjutsu are the *shuko* and *ashiko* hand and foot spiked bands. Used for digging or climbing up walls, cliffs, trees, ship sides, and even against the enemy himself; these clever implements were the invention of Togakure ninja. For many years, they were a secret weapon totally unknown to other ninjutsu schools.

As weapons, the spiked bands could protect the ninja's hand so that he could safely grab as assailant's razor-sharp sword and rip it out of his grip without injury. Coupled with kicks and strikes, the *shuko* and *ashiko* allowed the ninja to move inside an attacker's weapon range and subdue him. *Shuko* and *ashiko* bands were also highly effective against the enemy's unarmored body itself. Many times they were used to bring down attack dogs trained to maul intruders.

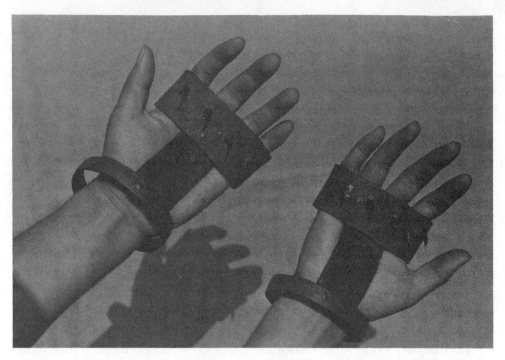

Shuko spiked bands for the hands (top) and *ashiko* bands for the feet (below).

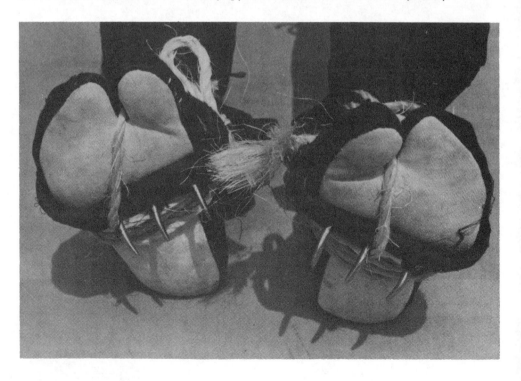

Grandmaster Masaaki Hatsumi uses the *shuko* spiked hand weapons to trap an attacker's sword and then counter-attack with a bone-jarring face slam.

Shuko and *ashiko* spiked bands can be seen in action in a defense against a sword slash attack. Dr. Hatsumi jams the attacker's downward cut with his left hand, and then stabilizes his restraining grip with his right in order to direct the assailant's blade safely to the side. Dr. Hatsumi then slams the *ashiko* beneath his right foot into the attacker's chest. With the *shuko* claws still firmly embedded in the attacker's wrist, the grandmaster then shifts to the attacker's right side, away from a possible left-handed grab. He next counterattacks with a punch to the ribs and a wrist throw that flips the assailant onto his back where he can be subdued.

Kusarigama and Kyoketsu Shoge
(Ninja Blade and Chain Weapons)

The long-range blade and chain weapons of the ninja combined cutting tools with the capability to strike or entangle an enemy at what he perceived to be a "safe" distance out of the way. Weighted chains, cords, and ropes of varying lengths were attached to sickles, daggers, and hooks, and served the historical ninja in many ways.

The *kusarigama* sickle and chain came to be used by samurai and peasant warriors alike. With its farming tool appearance, the *kusarigama* was a fairly unobtrusive weapon that could often be carried without arousing suspicion. Sickle portions of the tool could incorporate all sizes of blades and all lengths of handles, from small palm-size cutters to massive battlefield versions. Chain lengths gener-

ally ranged from nine to twelve feet.

The *kyoketsu shoge* is thought to have been developed before the more widely known *kusarigama*. Almost exclusively used by ninja, the *kyoketsu shoge* hooked blade and cord weapon had a multitude of useful applications. The blade could be used for pulling slashes as well as thrusting stabs. The eighteen-foot cord, sometimes made from women's or horses' hair for strength and resiliency, could be used for climbing, ensnaring an enemy, binding an enemy, setting traps, raising or lowering tools or equipment, as well as dragging loads. The ringed end could be tossed over protruding roof beams or tree limbs to secure the tool for climbing or scaling.

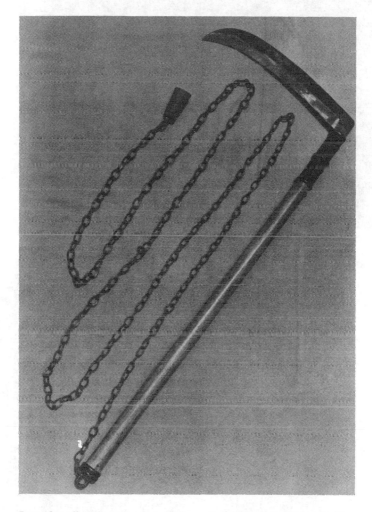

Long-handled *kusarigama* chain and sickle weapon, as used by
Togakure ryu ninja centuries ago.

Masaaki Hatsumi uses the *kusari-gama* with a flaming weight to reduce the sight of his adversary, making it easier to attain victory in the clash. The weighted chains were often used to deliver small explosive charges or fireballs.

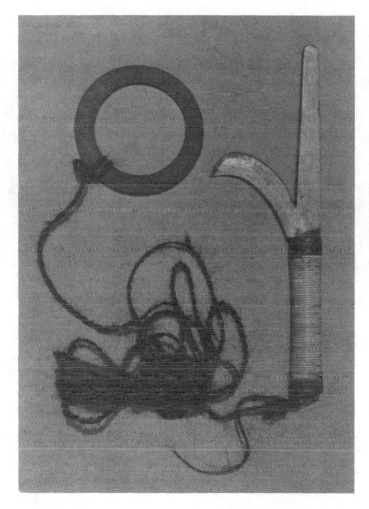

Ninjutsu's *kyoketsu shoge* cord and hooked blade weapon.
The tool could be used for cutting, binding, climbing, and
striking.

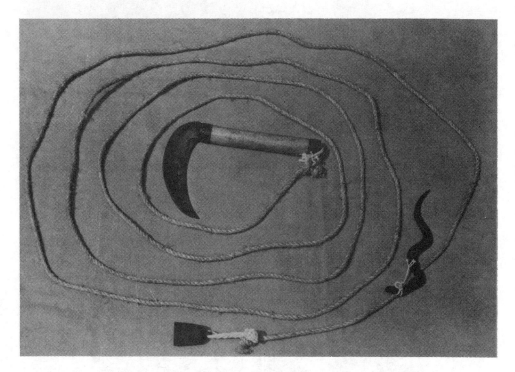

Another ninja innovation, the *mamukigama* cord and sickle weapon delivered a bound, terrified poisonous snake to the enemy's body. The enemy would then be so busy dealing with the snake bites, the he would be unable to counter the ninja as he advanced with his ripping sickle blade.

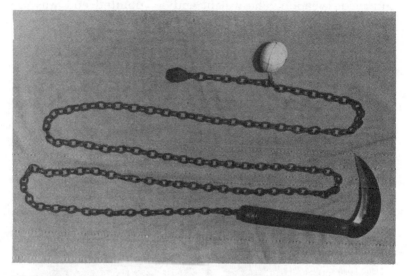

The egg-shell carrier of the *bakuhatsugama* could contain explosives, poison liquids, or blinding powers that would be released upon impact with the enemy's body.

A sword-wielding attacker gets a faceful of eye-stinging chemicals as the end of the *bakuhatsugama* chain cracks across his brow.

Grandmaster Hatsumi demonstrates the use of the *oh-gama* battlefield version of the ninja's chain and sickle weapon. The weight and chain were heavy enough to entangle and trip the legs of war-horses as well as strangle unmounted enemy warriors. The blade was used for slashing, and the pointed end was used for ramming thrusts.

Kusarifundo (Weighted Chain)

Closely related to the *kusari-gama* in application, although a close range weapon, is the *kusari-fundo* or weighted short chain. Ranging between eighteen and thirty inches in length and constructed of non-reflective etched steel, this flexible weapon can be used to strike, snare, or entangle the enemy or his weapon.

Fundamental striking attacks with the *kusarifundo*, as well as with the *kusarigama* and *kyoketsu shoge*, utilize the very end of the weight in motion in order to generate the most leverage and impact. Striking directions and trajectories include:

Tenchi furi — rising or falling vertical strikes.

Yoko furi — inward or outward horizontal strikes.

Happo furi — inward or outward diagonal strikes.

Naka furi — forward-shooting strikes.

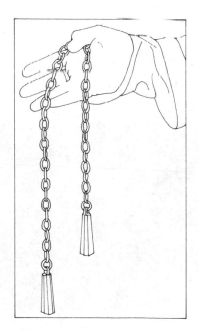

Kusarifundo weighted short chain weapon.

Masaaki Hatsumi applies a strangulation technique with the *kusari-* *fundo* short chain weapon.

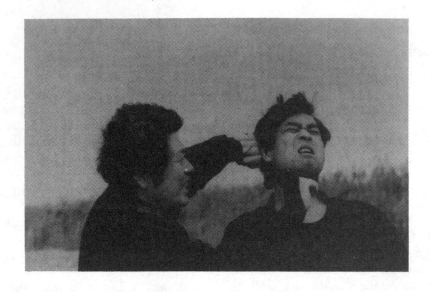

The grandmaster uses the *kusari-fundo* in an ensnaring move that immobilizes the attacker's arm while permitting an elbow slam to the chin.

Naginata and Bisen-Toh (Edged Halberds)

The *naginata* or Japanese halberd has been used since the Heian period of Japanese history. Though perhaps not a true halberd in the European sense of the word, the *naginata* was used as a long-range sword with slicing and stabbing capabilities. The weapon was primarily used by foot soldiers, who could take advantage of the reach to attack the legs of horses, or the samurai riding horses in battle. In later periods of Japanese history, the *naginata* came to be one of the primary weapons of the samurai woman, who was trained to use the long-range cutting tool with deadly skill in order to protect her house and family.

The *naginata* used by ninja were generally shorter in length and lighter in weight than the samurai battlefield version of the weapon. Often, the ninja *naginata* was a utilitarian blend of the individual ninja's short sword or dagger tied to the end of his six-foot *bo* staff for additional reach.

Unique in this history of Japanese weapons and war tools is the Togakure ryu *bisen-toh* or long-handled broadsword. The huge massive blade was so heavy that it could easily fall through the samurai armor and helmets of the times. According to legend, the Togakure ryu *bisen-toh* was introduced to Japanese culture by a recluse warrior who had fled his native China. This Chinese warrior, known as Tetsujo So, in his new home on the island of Honshu, was said to have trained Yoshiteru, who escaped to a cave in Izumo (now called Totori Prefecture) after defeat at the hands of Tadamitsu Fujiwara. Later generations of ninja further adapted the Chinese broadsword for use with indigenous Japanese war tools, and the *bisen-toh* went on to become a specialty weapon associated with the historical Togakure ryu ninjutsu tradition.

Due to the heavy weight of the *bisen-toh*, a system of using the body in motion, rather than the limbs alone, developed for using the unique combative tool. The fighter would firmly hold the handle, and then use body turns and footwork to employ the *bisen-toh* against the enemy. The weapon was used with the feeling of a battering ram or bludgeon, instead of a slicing or piercing weapon like the more conventional *naginata*.

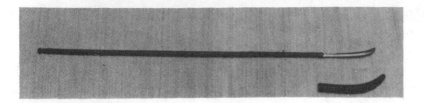

Naginata Japanese halberd.

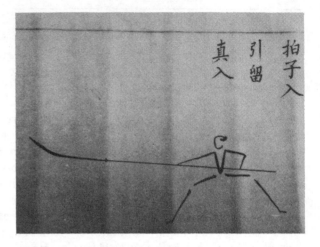

拍子入
引留
真入

Illustrations from the ancient manuscript depicting the effective use of the *naginata*.

Masaaki Hatsumi in battle-ready pose with the Togakure ryu ninjutsu *bisen-toh*.

Dr. Hatsumi uses the long handle of the *naginata*, along with dynamic body angling, to overcome his attacker. Note the sudden commit-ment of the grandmaster's weight as he drops to one knee to drive the blade into its target.

The weight of the *bisen-toh* long-handled sword in motion is enough to knock an attacker off his feet. Dr. Hatsumi steps forward with his right foot and leans into the swinging strike to topple the adversary. The grandmaster keeps right on going and ends up above the downed attacker, where he uses the sole of his foot to wedge the heavy blade into its target.

Also adopted from the Chinese war tool collection that came to the ninja of Japan at the fall of the T'ang Dynasty, the *ono* or battle ax was a weapon used to smash through castle gates, knock warriors off of their horses, or totally crush any attempt at combat with a lesser weapon. In this sequence, Shihan Tetsuji Ishizuka uses the *ono* against a swordsman.

Yumi and Ya (Ninja Bow and Arrows)

Normally carried in a bamboo tube for protection, the ninja *yumi* bow and *ya* arrows were much shorter, in fact about half the length, than the conventional longbows of Japanese troops. The shorter bow was much easier to carry and conceal, and its reduced power was not really a problem in that most ninja's bow and arrow work was done from relatively close ranges and not across vast battlefields.

In addition to being used for sniping, assassination, or ambush purposes, the ninja bow and arrow was relied on heavily for signalling, creating diversions, setting fires, scattering troops, and illuminating night scenes. Specially constructed arrows carried bombs, whistles, flares, message capsules, poison tips, the end of an escape rope, or anything else that a ninja might want to move through the air.

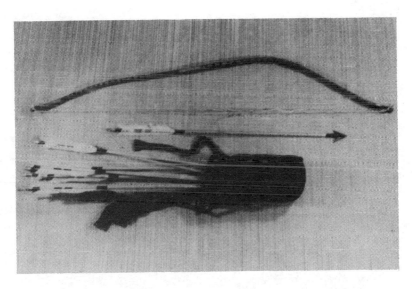

Ninja *yumi* bow and pouch of short *ya* arrows.

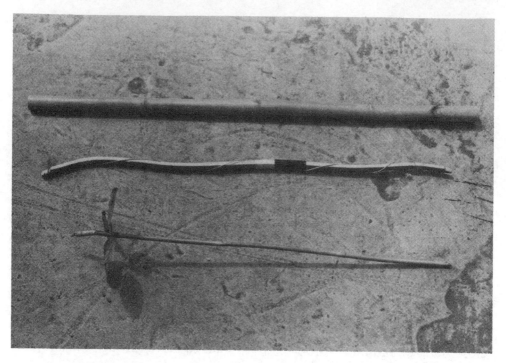

Ninja bow, arrow, and bamboo tube carrying case.

Ninja arrows containing explosives, flares, and noisemakers.

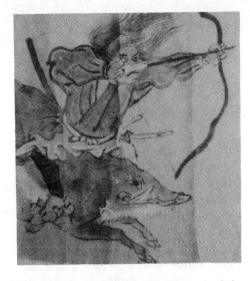

Manuscript illustration showing ninja firing an arrow from the back of a running boar.

Firing position for the compact ninja bow and arrow.

Fukiya (Blowguns)

The ninja blowgun was used for silent killing, creating confusion in the enemy's household, alarming the enemy's animals, and signaling. Fairly short for convenience in carrying, the ninjutsu blowgun was a close range weapon, and was accurate within approximately twenty feet. Often disguised by being built into flutes, canes, and umbrellas, the blowgun could be carried into the area of operation without the difficulty of avoiding suspicion. After use, they were just as easily carried away from the scene.

Darts were constructed of paper cones and steel slivers. Poison or secret messages could also be affixed to the blowgun darts.

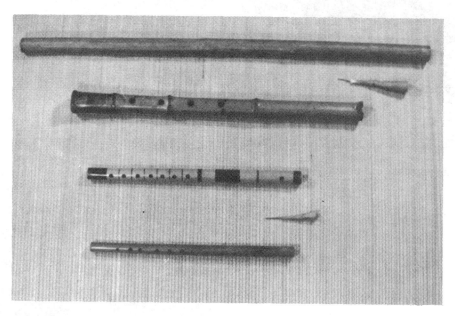

Ninja *fukiya* blowguns built in Japanese flutes and cane tubes.

Ninja firing compact bow and arrows and
blowgun from concealing brush.

A long range ninja blowgun fired from a high vantage point.

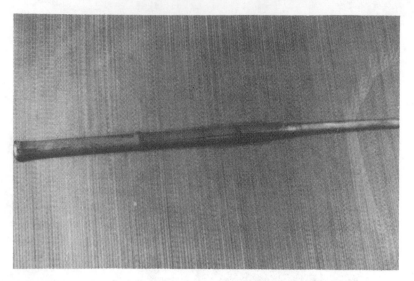

With this pressure activated poison water blowgun, hydraulic action forces a stream of eye-irritant or flammable liquid at the approaching enemy.

Poison water blowgun in use.

Toami jutsu (Fish Nets)

The ninja could use any item that would work to carry out his intentions of survival. The net was a common enough item in fishing villages, and could be used to en- snare and control multiple attackers. Nets were also rigged up as traps in wooded areas as well as in castle corridors.

Yari (Spears)

As with most other weapons employed by the historical Togakure ninja, the *yari* or spear of ninjutsu has a design somewhat different from that of the spears traditionally used by the samurai foot soldiers. Japanese spears were generally hand held and used for piercing or stabbing attacks to exposed areas between the plates of the samurai armor. Spears were rarely thrown. Long wooden shafts were tipped with straight double-edged or triple-edged blades.

Togakure ryu ninja more often utilized a unique spear weapon called *kamayari*, which was a blend of characteristics from the spear and hooked or sickle weapons. In addition to serving as a long-range stabbing and piercing weapon, ninjutsu's *kamayari* could also be used for a wide variety of other purposes. The hooked end could be extended up over a tree limb, castle wall, or ship side, transforming the *kamayari* into a climbing tool. Ninja could also reach from one tree to another or from a roof to a tree, with the *kamayari* and then swing away from the area on the weapon. The ninja could conceal himself in a high tree or low growing shrubs and reach out with the hook to snag passing enemies. In fighting clashes, the hooked spear could be used to catch and direct the assailant's weapon arm or weapon itself. The *kamayari* was also used as a pole for carrying baggage or equipment, barring doors, or catching fish.

Kamayari hooked spears of ninjutsu.

A ninja uses the *kamayari* hooked over a tree limb to swing across an open space.

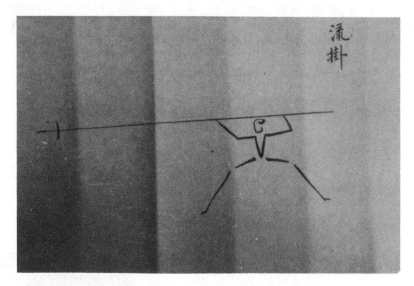

Technique illustration from an ancient scroll.

In a series of subtle push-pull trade-offs, Dr. Hatsumi gains control of an attacker's sword arm. The grandmaster pushes the spear towards the swordsman's face. He responds by deflecting the grandmaster's spear. Dr. Hatsumi then hooks the deflecting sword, which causes the swordsman to pull his sword away to avoid having it trapped. Dr. Hatsumi then follows the sword with his spear, gaining control of the assailant's arms while shifting into close range with his footwork. While keeping the sword away from himself, Dr. Hatsumi executes a rising footsweep with his left foot, which lifts the attacker's right leg off the ground. As the attacker hits the ground, the point of Dr. Hatsumi's *kamayari* moves from the swordsman's wrists to his throat.

A ninja uses a *hashigoyari* "ladder spear," equipped with peg steps that can be inserted into holes along the shaft to scale a wall. The tip of the spear has a hooked point for snaring tree limbs during climbs, and for grabbing enemies during combat. Holes along the shaft are drilled at fixed distances from each other so that the *hashigoyari* could also be used as a measuring device during reconnaissance missions.

Tetsubishi and Igadama (Caltrops)

Dried water chestnuts, or *hishi* in the Japanese language, were used as miniature caltrops by ninja of old. In a rural farming area, the natural plant products would not arouse any suspicion, although they could be put into action as quite effective anti-pursuit devices. When strewn across the wooden veranda of a ninja house or along a path leading to the house, the tiny pointed objects disappeared in the darkness of night. Their form, however, provided a thorn sticking straight up no matter which way they tumbled. When stepped on by the unsuspecting, the tough thorn would pierce right through a straw sandel or cotton-soled *tabi* and produce screams of pain by surprised pursuers or intruders.

In later years, the natural plant product was replaced by steel versions known as *tetsubishi*. Constructed out of twisted iron or steel, the foot spikes could penetrate a foot several inches, and when barbed on the ends, could not be removed easily so the victim could resume the chase. When the pursuer went down, he stayed down until a surgeon could tend to him.

Igadama were spiked balls of iron or steel that could be left scattered on the floor or ground to slow down pursuers or could be thrown through the air at assailants. These weapons were effective for the defense of ninja houses in that they did not readily appear to be weapons and could be left in all parts of the house in case they needed to be hurled at the face of an intruder.

Hishi dried water chestnut foot spikes and a convenient carrying case for night missions.

Steel and iron *tetsubishi* foot spikes, capable of deeply penetrating a foot.

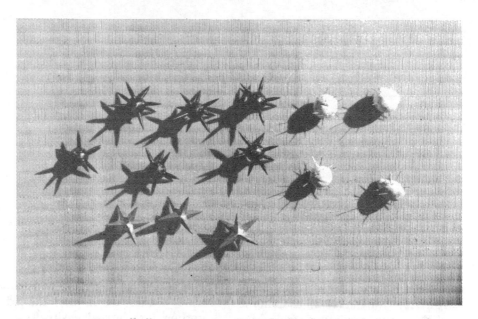

Ingadama, or "Iga balls," spiked steel or iron spheres that could be left scattered on the ground or could be hurled at attackers as they approached (left). Also shown are *dokubari* versions of the same weapon concept (right). Poisoned needles were jammed into plant fiber cores and left behind for the foot of the unsuspecting.

Illustration from a historical manuscript describing the construction and use of caltrops for slowing pursuers.

Shuriken (Throwing Blades)

Perhaps the most well-known and characteristic weapon of the ninja is the *shuriken* or throwing blade. Historically, the ninja used *shuriken* that covered a wide variety of designs based upon two fundamental weapon types. *Hira shuriken* were flat plates with anywhere from three to as many as eight points radiating from the center. *Bo shuriken* were straight blades with either one or two points. Each type of blade had its own characteristic way of being handled and thrown.

The technique of throwing stones to defeat an enemy has existed from ancient times. As the art of warfare evolved, the somewhat crude method of hurling stones was transformed into the technique of throwing flat iron plates, as is recorded in famous volumes from Japan's history, such as the *Heike Monogatari* or *Yoshitsune-ki.* The art of throwing flat iron plates had a great influence on the development of the art of accurately throwing knives and other straight bladed weapons.

One of the specialties of the historical Togakure ryu was the use of a four-pointed throwing blade known as a *senban shuriken.* Four points radiated out from a square center hole, giving the *senban shuriken* a diamond-like ap-

pearance. The steel was heat treated and hammered thin for lightness and more effective cutting, in contrast to the heavy, chisel-like toy immitations available from American martial arts equipment dealers today. The *senban shuriken* were thin enough that nine blades could be stacked together and carried easily in a concealed pocket inside of the ninja's jacket lapel.

To begin training with the *shuriken*, whether the straight blade or star shaped variety, it is important to first get used to the feel of properly releasing the blade for flight. In this initial stage, the target need not be more than three feet away. Begin by lightly tossing the blade into the wooden surface of the target without any concern for distance or power. Work to develop the feeling that the blade seems to slide out of your hand by itself, rather than a sensation of you slamming the blade into the target. A light tensing of the wrist at the last second, just as the point of the blade is aimed at the target, will tend to encourage the feeling for a proper release of the blade. The throwing arm should be aimed right at the target point at the moment of the *shuriken's* release.

Senban shuriken can be stacked in the left hand and pulled off one by one for throwing with the right hand. *Bo shuriken* can be held in a bundle in the left hand and pulled out one at a time for throwing with the right hand. The *shuriken* are held lightly in the hand, with the fingerips gently holding them in place for throwing.

Once a proper feel for throwing has been developed, more distance can be added to the target. When farther away from the target, power must be generated by moving the body with the throw as well as snapping the hand and forearm in one movement. The body can rock back and forth with each draw and throw, or the rear foot can shift into forward position with the throw. The feeling of body weight behind the throw will be similar to that of effectively using the body weight in motion to generate power for punches in the ninja's *taijutsu* unarmed combat system.

To learn *shuriken* throwing is also learning how to avoid being hit with the *shuriken* as well. In the technique of *totoku hiyoshi*, ninja are trained to slip by or knock away *shuriken* thrown at them. A sword can also be used to slap flying *shuriken* out of the air.

A four-pointed Togakure ryu *senban shuriken* flies through the air.

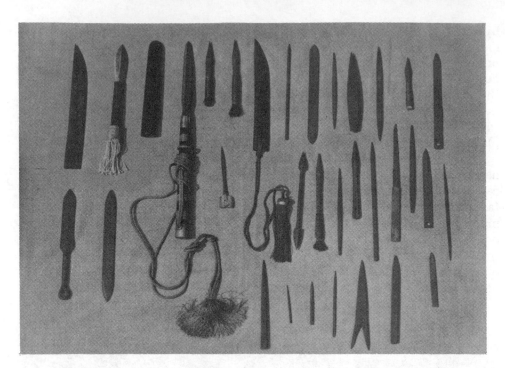

Bo shuriken straight throwing blades.

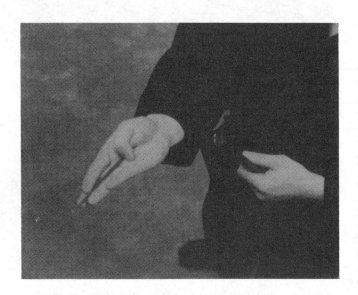

Gripping the *bo shuriken* for throwing.

Hira shuriken flat throwing plates and star knives.

Tsubute clubbing throwing missiles.

The flat plate *shuriken* are held lightly in the hand, with the fingertips gripping the outermost edges of the points when throwing. *Shuriken* can also be held tightly in the hand and used as close-range cutting weapons, instead of being thrown.

Senban shuriken carried in a pack of nine, concealed inside a ninja's jacket.

Dr. Hatsumi demonstrates the *senban shuriken* horizontal throw. Note how the grandmaster uses his body weight in motion to generate power for the blade's flight.

Gripping and throwing the *itaken* straight bladed *shuriken*, Dr. Hatsumi uses a forward step to propel the wide blade towards the target in front of him.

A forward view of the step-through *shuriken* throw. Note the simultaneity of the step and the extension of the throwing arm occur at the same time.

Tree trunks and upright planes of wood make good targets for training with the *shuriken* throwing blades.

Totoku hiyoshi techniques train the ninja to avoid injury from *shuriken* blades thrown at him by enemies.

Dr. Hatsumi lights and throws an *endokuken* poison smoke *shuriken*. The concealed ninja must expose his position in order to avoid inhaling the noxious fumes.

Metsubushi ("Sight Removers" or Eye Blinders)

The ninja agent was almost always sure to be outnumbered if he or she were discovered or captured by guards in their area of clandestine operation. Therefore, the ninja had to develop an effective way to reduce the advantage of a larger group of enemies.

Metsubushi or "slight removers" caused the ninja's attackers to hesitate in their advance or proved a screen to cover the ninja's escape.

This created and reinforced the legends of the ninja's ability to disappear at will. Hollowed out egg shells or nut hulls as well as paper packets were used to carry the blinding powders and deliver them against the enemy. The powder itself could be a slow-burning explosive or could be a mixture of fine grit, ashes, ground pepper, and nettle hairs.

Dr. Hatsumi stuns two attackers with an explosive surprise.

Metsubushi sight removers and *senban shuriken* throwing stars carried in a concealed pocket inside the ninja's jacket.

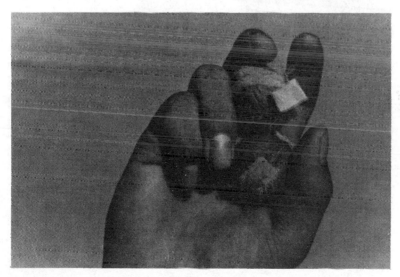

Walnut hulls emptied and refilled with blinding powder for use against an enemy's close quarters attack.

Hollowed egg shells with wax plugs, loaded with blinding powder.

A sword-wielding attacker gets a faceful of the ninja's *metsubushi* blinding powder.

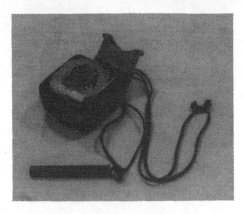

This ornate *metsubushi* device gave a ninja the ability to subdue his enemy with a single outgoing breath. With the attached plug pulled, the mouthpiece permitted a stream of air to send a cloud of pepper out the front of the weapon and into the eyes of an attacker. Because the device did not permanently damage the victim on which it was used, this type of *metsubushi* was often used by police during the relatively peaceful Tokugawa era in Japan.

SPECIAL TRAINING

The art of ninjutsu employs a broad collection of esoteric knowledge that provides the basis for the ninja's unique approach to life, understanding, and the prevention of danger. More than a system of physical tricks for espionage and combat; ninjutsu is a total way of life in which all aspects of the environment, all levels of consciousness, and total perspective of one's understandings are blended together to provide a life harmonious with the playing out of the universe.

The ninja embodies the concept of "enduring" the universe in three ways. *Mi wo shinobu* provides a body that is conditioned, trained, and maintained for physical endurance. The conscious mind of *kokoro wo shinobu* is tempered, broadened, and directed for mental perseverance. With *shiki wo shinobu*, vision and realization are focused internally and externally at the same time for spiritual fortitude, the forbearance of total knowledge that comes with wisdom. Unlike the conventional martial skills that can be learned by the body and brain in a relatively short period of time, the total life skills of ninjutsu are acquired through a lifetime of diligent training, observation, and personal development that takes the practitioner far beyond the qualities of a mere human fighting machine and moves him or her forward to a state of enlightenment.

Heavily influenced by the Indian, Tibetan, and Chinese mystic teachings of *mikkyo*, *tantra*, *ekkyo* (I Ching), and other methods of experiencing and interpreting the will and flow of the universe, ninjutsu tactics and techniques often incorporate the symbolism of nature to provide inspiration for practical application. In somewhat of a parallel to the right and left hands, two distinct sets or groups of symbols are used in harmony and coordination with each other to suggest how things "operate" (the real of material reality), and how things "are" (the realm of ultimate truth). Though the two realms do exist at exactly the same place and time, they can appear to be different because of a limited scope of vision on the part of the viewer. They are in reality two different views of the same identical process.

From the realm of ultimate truth comes the *go dai*, or "five elemental manifestations." The progression of *ku*, *fu*, *ka*, *sui*, and *chi* (the void, wind, fire, water, and earth) depicts the creation of the universe, and symbolizes the ways that physical matter manifests itself as formless atomic potential, gasses, combustive energy, liquids, and solids. This series decribes how things *are*.

From the real of material reality comes the *go gyo* series, or "five primary elements," which describes how things inter-relate and *operate*. *Chi*, *sui*, *ka*, *moku*, and *kin* (earth, water, fire wood, and metal) continuously work and interact to create and then destroy each other. Just as water nurtures the growing tree which is then brought down by the metal blade and consumed by the fire to produce the dust of the earth, the five elements can also be seen as they operate symbolically in the regulation of an individual's health, and in the unfolding of life events.

The historical ninja used the knowledge of how all the pieces of nature fit and complement each other to develop what became known as the *go ton po* method of escape concealment using the five elements. Because of the ninja's Taoist heritage from Chinese teachers over a thousand years ago, a working familiarity with nature and natural laws became the theory behind the application of ninjustu escape skills. *Do* (or *chi*) *Ton jutsu* or earth methods involve the use of rocks, soil, and land contours to aid the ninja escape. *Sui ton jutsu* or water methods involve the use of *sui ki* equipment for moving across the surface of ponds, rivers, swamps, and moats, as well as unique gear for remaining submerged under water. *Ka ton jutsu* includes the use of fire, smoke, and explosives as diversionary devices. *Ka ki* firearms, grenades, and land mines also fit into this classification. *Moku ton jutsu* methods make use of trees, foliage, plants, and *to ki* rope and ladder climbing equipment as means for escape and survival. *Kin ton jutsu* employs the characteristics of metal, and incorporates the use of a wide range of *kai ki* tools for gaining access to enemy strongholds.

Don ton jutsu earth concealment techniques allow the ninja to blend into the ground until the opportune moment for action.

Using rocks and boulders for concealment or escape coverage is another aspect of the *do ton jutsu* earth utilization technique.

Dr. Hatsumi practices one of the ninja methods for running. Here he crosses a narrow strip of ground bordered by saturated rice fields.

Another ninjutsu running practice, the crossed leg sideways gait allows the ninja to move rapidly along narrow passages, the ridges of hills, or rooftop spines. The hands are rhythmically thrown outward for balance whenever the feet cross each other as the ninja moves forward or backward.

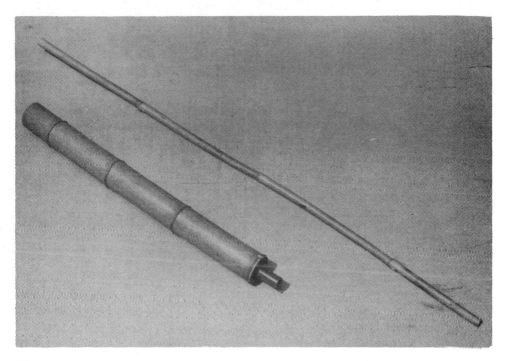

Ninja breathing tubes for waiting or working underwater.

A ninja about to submerge where water plants can conceal
the protruding tip of his breathing tube.

A ninja emerges from his submerged hiding place and moves like a shadow up the wall of the enemy's outer defense barrier.

Ninjutu's *mizu gumo* water crossing device is an inflatable seat that surrounds the ninja's hips and suspends him in the water. The air pouches were made of rabbit skin on top with horse hide underneath.

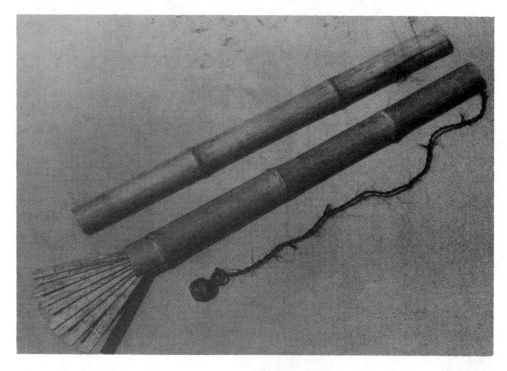

The *Shinobi kai* collapsable oar for use with ninja water crossing devices.

Ninja using the *mizu gumo* water seat.

Suspension properties of the *mizu gumo* water seat as seen from below the water's surface.

Kama ikada water crossing device of nin-jutsu.

Taru ikada flotation pots for crossing shallow waterways.

Hasami bune collapsible float for transporting equipment across water.

Tsugi bune collapsible boat. Each member of the ninja team could carry his own piece of the boat. The individual sections, which appeared to be nothing more than storage boxes, could then be joined to form the actual boat.

About to vanish behind a wall of flame, a ninja demonstrates the concept of *ka ton jutsu* as a means of using fire to facilitate an escape.

Flaming shuriken throwing stars, thrown into an enemy's camp area to startle and set distracting fires.

Historical ninja of the Togakure ninjutsu ryu could rely on the shocking technique of *onibi no jutsu*, the "art of the demon's fire," to overcome superstitious adversaries. Fireworks and flammable chemicals coupled with carved wooden demon masks made the ninja a terrifying sight.

Iburi dashi method of "smoking out" the enemy forces the adversary to choose between capture and suffocation.

Dokuenjutsu use of poisoned smoke to keep an enemy attacker at bay or chase him away in search of safer breathing areas.

Ninja matchlock pistol.

Tanegashima long rifle used by Warring States Period ninja.

Ohzutsu wooden mortar used by Togakure ryu ninja.

Ohzutsu being carried into position for firing.

A ninja team fires the *ohzutsu* mortar from a covering of young bamboo.

Sodezutsu hand held small cannon.

In chain mail armor, Masaaki Hatsumi poses with a *sodezutsu* hand cannon and *uchidake* fire-staring device.

Wakizaski teppo, a unique concealed weapon that hides a single shot handgun in the other casings of a typical *wakizashi* short sword.

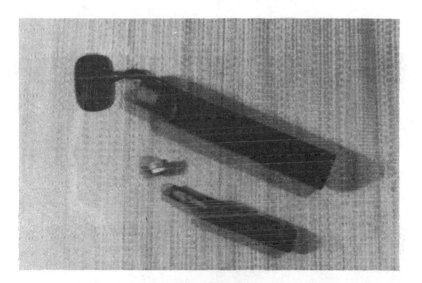

Used to light fuses, set fires, and provide warmth, the ninja's *uchidake* contained embers inside of several bamboo tube layers.

Nagedeppo explosive grenades, thrown by hand or projected by slings at the enemy.

Buried under the ground's surface, *umebi* land mines were constructed to explode when stepped on by the unsuspecting.

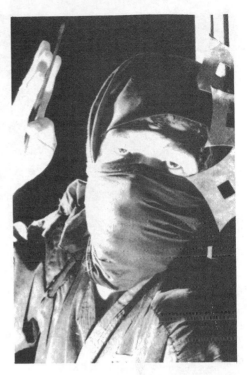

Ninjutsu's *kin ton jutsu* metal escape attitudes could utilize iron and steel fighting implements that were unique to the ninja. The Togakure ryu *senban shuriken* are good examples of the creative use of metal as a means of facilitating escape.

Polished steel mirrors could be used for signaling allies and other team members, or for blinding approaching enemies and their horses.

Kunai digging and leverage tools (top) and *tsubo giri* boring tools (bottom) from the ninja's *kai ki* implements for access to enemy strongholds.

Kiri single-pointed pick borers, and the *tsubo giri* in application.

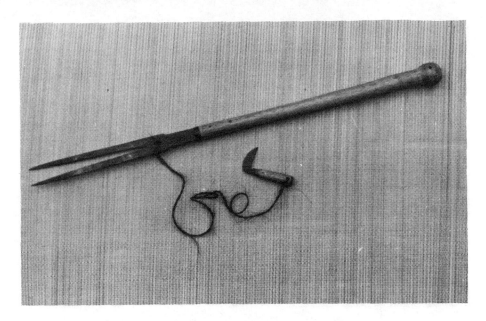

Tobi kunai for gaining access through barred gates.

Shikoro thin-bladed saws for going through wooden doors and walls.

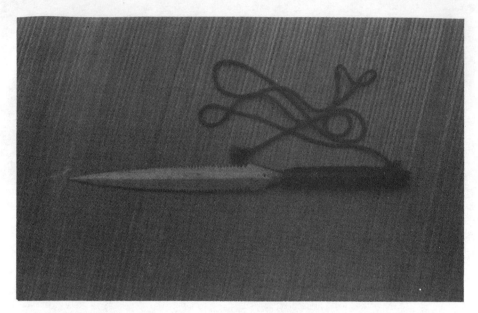

Yajiri heavy-bladed saw.

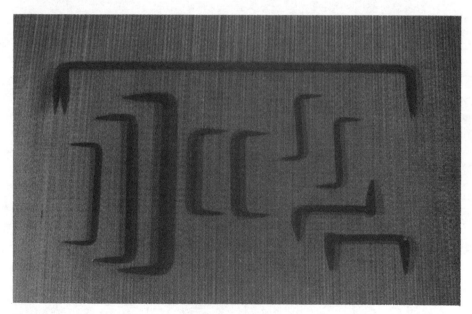

Kasugai iron clamps for holding doors closed in order to prevent entry or escape.

Gando portable lighting tool, in which a candle is always held in an upright position, regardless of the angle at which the shield is held.

Three-foot length of coarse black cloth, used for muffling the sounds of the ninja's *kai ki* entrance tools. The cloth could also be used as a face mask or a water filter.

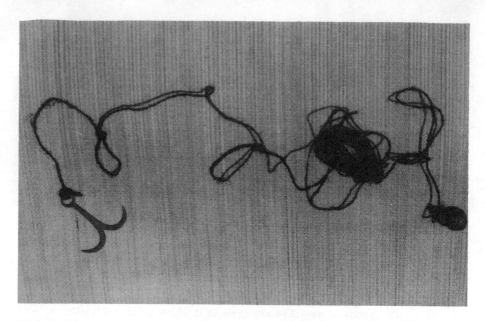

Musubi bashigo "loop ladder" single cable climbing device. The tied loops could be grabbed by the hand, or could be used to support the foot for extended periods of time while digging or boring through a wall or fortification.

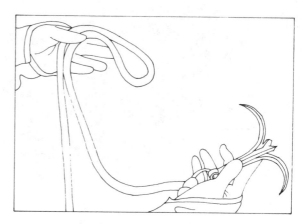

The loops are formed by folding over the cord and tying a simple knot in such a way as to leave an extended loop.

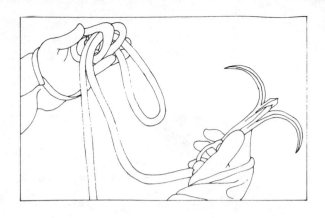

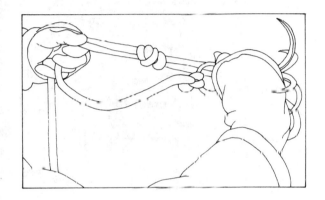

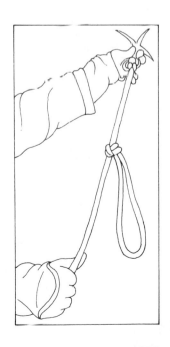

Ninja ladders from the author's collection. From left to right, *kumo bashigo* (cloud ladder), *kuda bashigo* (tube ladder), *tsuri bashigo* (hanging ladder) with anchoring hooks along its length, and two styles of *tobi bashigo* ("leaping" ladders). Note that the construction permits fast and easy unfolding and collapsing.

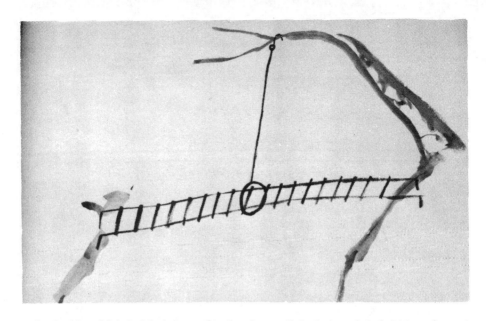

Taka bashigo (high ladder) from the *densho* scroll depicting ninja *kai ki* equipment for gaining access to the enemy's stronghold. The actual tool, used for crossing over high open spaces, is pictured below.

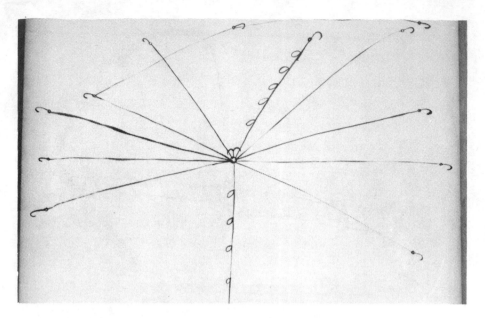

Densho illustration of the *kumo bashigo* (spider ladder) and the actual tool from Dr. Hatsumi's personal collection.

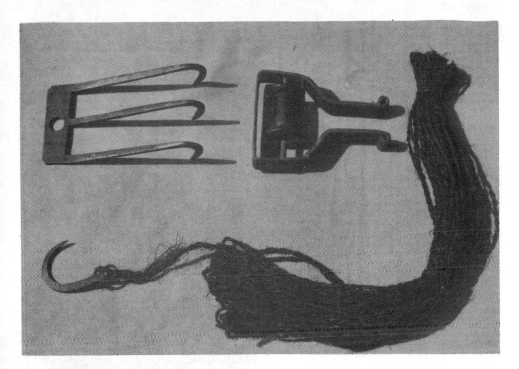

The *kasha* pulley and rope were used to quickly move ninja and equipment over broad open spaces. Perhaps most often used as a pre-planned escape route, the rope could be used to speed ninja agents away from an enemy castle tower.

A ninja prepares to launch himself forward on the *kasha* pulley escape device.

Shihan Fumio Manaka demonstrates nin-jutsu lateral rope progression from tree to tree.

Moku ton jutsu techniques of escape and concealment make use of trees and shrubs to protect the ninja.

Ninja disappear into treetops above the
normal sight line of travellers on a road.

Ninja gain access to treetops by techniques of *shoten no jutsu,* or "climbing to the heavens." The training begins with gentle slopes and then moves on to steeper planes and finally to vertical surfaces

In his snow colored suit, the ninja could blend in with his surroundings to conceal himself while scouting out the enemy's location.

Specially constructed *yuki waragi* snow
sandals allow the ninja to move confi-
dently, even in loose or wet snow. Short
lengths of bamboo secured to the under-
side of the footwear grip into the snow
underfoot.

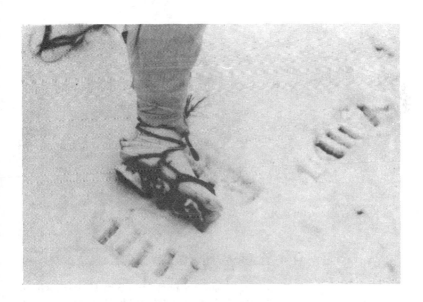

Togakure ryu *shuko* spiked handbands wrapped for blending with the snow during winter usage. The cloth wrapping also insulates the ninja's hand from contact with frozen iron construction of the climbing claws.

A ninja uses an icicle weapon to dispatch an enemy in this creative application of the principles of nature.

Techniques of *taijutsu* unarmed combat as well as weapon defenses and stealth walking are practiced on the frozen surface of a pond in order to develop the proper feel of using the body motion, and not the feet or shoulders alone, to deliver power.

Kunoichi (Female Ninja)

Kunoichi or female ninja made up an important part of the historical ninja families and clans of Japan. In alignment with the pragmatic tendency of ninjutsu to stress the most effective employment of tools, the female warriors were trained in ways of warfare that most appropriately capitalized on their own unique features and strengths. Tactics of psychological warfare and the manipulating of the enemy's mind and perception were specialties of the *kunoichi*. The female ninja could often use her own femininity as a means of getting the enemy to drop his guard and overlook her potential as a destructive adversary. Women in feudal Japan were often underestimated in terms of their capabilities for power, and this permitted the *kunoichi* to pose as one of the household staff in order to gain easy access to the very center of the enemy stronghold.

The psychic and intuitive powers of female ninja were also relied upon when determining plans for future action based on the most likely developments in the enemy's strategy.

The women's education stressed the use of smaller close-range weapons rather than the larger battle implements, because the female *kunoichi* was more often used from within the enemy's midst than from without. Concealed daggers, blinders, drugs, strangulation tools, explosives, and throwing blades were more often used than swords, staffs, or spears. The female ninja could also usually rely on her adversary to be susceptible to the appearance of weakness in order to facilitate her move into range for action. Tears, subservience, sexuality, and feigned fear were all effective ruses for the female ninja.

Mariko Hatsumi carries a ninja dagger and smoke grenade beneath the cat in her arms. As well as concealing the ninja gear, the cat could also serve as a potent distraction weapon itself when thrown into the face of an unsuspecting intruder.

Kimono sleeve dagger carried by *kunoichi* female ninja.

Innocent enough in appearance, this typical tea-making kit actually transports the *kunoichi's senban shuriken* and a small explosives pack for blowing open a door.

Flowers being carried across a courtyard or through a marketplace would not usually draw much attention. In this case, a concealed assassination weapon for a female ninja.

In this sequence, a female ninja uses an upward swing with the end of a *han-bo*, or "half *bo*" cane, to smash the wrist of an attacker and knock his knife out of his grip. She then circles around away from his hands and attacks his knee structure to force the attacker to the ground. A ramming strike to the temple incapacitates the downed assailant.

229

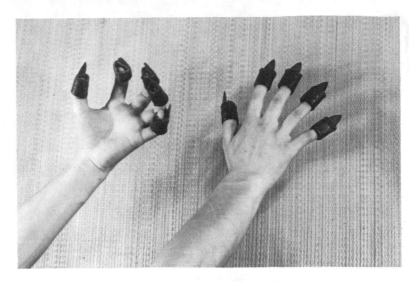

Leather and steel *neko te* fingertip weapons turn a *kunoichi's* hand into a death-dealing claw.

Kiai (Energy Attuning)

The word *ki* in the Japanese language is defined as the universal dynamic force, the energy behind the "spirit" of everything in existence or potentially in existence. *Ai* is the root form for Japanese words that translate as "harmony," "coming together," and "associating." As interpreted by the *densho* scrolls compiled by the former head masters of the Togakure ryu, the concept of *kiai* is literally translated as "harmonizing with the dynamic force of the universe." *Kiai-jutsu*, therefore, is the technique of being in harmony with this dynamic force in order to act and react with what is appropriate. It means attuning with the total flow of energies and happenings of which we are a part. All the individual pieces and aspects merge as one flow.

In many contemporary martial training systems, the concept of *kiai* has unfortunately been reduced to a mere shout accompanying aggressive action. There is of course a physiological benefit to the *kiai* shout, though the true concept of *kiai* goes far beyond shouting alone. Energy naturally produces noise with its release. Crackling fires, thunder claps, fire cracker blasts, and electrical short circuits are all examples of "*kiai* shouts" from nature. The energy generated and expelled with a lunge, a kick, a throw, or a slash naturally creates a rush of air from the lungs in a similar manner. This rush of air coupled with the momentary tension of the body, including the throat, produces the roaring growl of the true *kiai* shout.

Beginning students of karate, jodo, and kendo can be made to shout with the delivery of techniques as a means of learning proper breathing and mental focus. The expelled air prevents the habit of nervously holding the breath with a strike application. The violent noise temporarily diverts the student from worrying about being hit or thrown with a counter technique as he makes his move. The shout can also divert the attention of the student's opponent for a crucial fraction of a second. Until the *kiai* release of breath becomes a natural part of the fighter, however, it will remain merely an uncomfortable training hall tool, used only in the *dojo*, and will only contribute to the feeling of artificiality in the martial arts practice session. However, the training hall must reflect the actual world if one is working at learning a combat-oriented fighting art such as ninjutsu, and there can be no room for any inhibiting factors whatsoever. Without a feeling of natural spontaneity, a *kiai* shout is a worthless endeavor. Without thoroughly understanding the point of the shout, and lots of uninhibited practice, naturalness will never be reached.

To create the most effective *kiai* shout, use a low, open throated vowel sound, and avoid high-pitched shrieks or squealing noises. You want a harsh, totally commited roar, and not a scream of fright. The shout is a vocalization of your emotions, and comes up from the diaphragm instead of from the back of your throat.

Based on natural emotional conditions, there are four general types of *kiai*, as observed by the past masters of our ninja tradition.

ATTACKING SHOUT

The attacking *kiai* shout is a fierce explosive noise that causes the adversary to drop his concentration momentarily. Grounded from the lower abdomen, the shout resonates through the body to startle, terrify, and overwhelm the enemy. Though there are no specific words associated with the attacking shout, a low, drawn-out, almost growling "ehy!" sound is typical for native speakers of Japanese.

REACTING SHOUT

The reacting *kiai* shout is a heavy, intense noise that creates a sense of disappointment in the enemy as his tactics are thwarted. From the tightened midsection, the shout hisses up through the body to accompany the mental charge upon discovering the enemy's hidden weapon, or successfully avoiding his attack. The hollow sounding exhalation usually takes a 'toh!" form with Japanese speaking practitioners.

VICTORIOUS SOUND

The victorious shout is a boisterous, triumphant noise that cele-brates the overpowering of the enemy. The ringing shouts come from the solar plexus with the exuberance of a laugh, to discourage and bewilder the adversary after a series of blows have been dealt. "Yah!" or "yoh!" sounds are natural for Japanese speakers, although the sounds have no word meanings. Native speakers of other languages will produce noises more fitting with their own tonal qualities.

"SHADOW" SHOUT

The fourth shout, or "shadow *kiai*," is not necessarily a vocal shout at all, but rather a total plunging of the body, mind, and feelings into the destiny of the fight. If any sound at all were emitted, it might take a "uhmn" sort of quality as this *kiai* form takes over the ninja's fighting presence by spontaneously blending the characteristics of the attacking, reacting, and victorious *kiai* shouts in the ninja's consciousness. This is the highest level of involvement. Attacks are used at the crucial moment before a defense is needed, so that the attack is in reality a protection. In touch with the adversary's intentions, there is no surprise and therefore no need to react, in the true sense of the word. Finally, even as the victor, one is in danger, in that by defeating another, the desire of revenge is created in the vanquished. Comparisons and classifications fade in their distinctiveness as you immerse yourself in the totalness of the fight, oblivious to the past or future. The only sound left is your breathing in rhythm with the events transpiring from second to second.

The key to effective self-protection is the total involvement in the activity from moment to moment. When the *kiai* takes over your personality, the very intensity of what you are doing and thinking will dominate the moment entirely. Roaring yells are produced naturally at appropriate times. You are not merely imitating a person in a fight; you have switched your personality to the feelings of actual combat. You have totally become your intention.

An experience of my teacher Toshitsugu Takamatsu illustrates the effectiveness of the living *kiai*. Years ago when studying under his teacher, the training hall was disturbed by a huge student from the Sekiguchi ryu bujutsu school. The big man issued a challenge to the Togakure ryu dojo of grandmaster Toda. As Toda Sensei's highest ranking student, Toshitsugu Takamatsu would naturally have been the one to take on the Sekiguchi fighter. Before the match could even be acknowledged, however, a junior student of Takamatsu Sensei leaped to his feet and insisted on meeting the challenger. The student was older than Takamatsu Sensei, though not has highly ranked, and his enthusiasm and commitment won him the right to face the man who questioned the ability of Toda Sensei and his senior student Takamatsu Sensei. This was not at all the usual procedure for handling such confrontations.

The student moved to the fighting area without hesitation and leaped up onto the hardwood floor with a roaring shout and a thunderous stamping of feet. Though an older man, the student's wide shoulders, scar-crossed face, and neck with its bulging veins gave him a fierce look. Even though the student was not really a good fighter, according to Takamatsu Sensei, he must have seemed convincing to the Sekiguchi ryu man, who visibly flinched backwards in shock as the Togakure dojo representative headed for him without any formalities. Realizing what he had done without even thinking, the Sekiguchi student held up his hands and then bowed in defeat before his opponent had gotten half way across the floor towards him. When questioned by Toda Sensei, the Sekiguchi ryu fighter replied that he had been totally taken aback by the little man's scream of indignation and the demonic look on his face. Though probably a better skilled technician than the Togakure ryu man, the intruder had been soundly defeated by the power of pure intention alone.

The harmony with the universal force implied in the concept of *kiai* is in no way limited to the body of each individual alone. As in the foregoing story, we can often feel the force of intentions themselves, far ahead of any physical action that may involve us subsequently. Even if no actions follow, we have no doubt that we have experienced the other person's intention. We know they were committed and that they later chose not to follow through with their actions. This bending of the *ki* force is known as *sakki*, or "force of the killer." It is the feeling that our intentions project when we are determined to destroy someone else. Animals as well as humans project this *sakki* as a natural part of their determination to overtake another being. In real life self-protection situations, the ability to blend in with the *ki* of another and pick up the *sakki* directed at the target is a crucial skill for emerging alive from the conflict. That skill is perhaps the most significant difference that separates ninjutsu training from the more popular sport martial arts training.

Togakure ryu master instructor Tsunehisa Tanemura waits calmly in the *seiza* kneeling posture as Dr. Hatsumi moves into position behind him. Tsunehisa Tanemura then tumbles to his left as he picks up the feeling of *sakki*, or the "killing intention," just in time to avoid the downward *tenchi giri* slice of the sword behind him.

From the *seiza* kneeling posture, ninjutsu master instructor Shihan Fumio Manaka maintains meditative calm while grandmaster Masaaki Hatsumi takes his position behind him. At the instant Dr. Hatsumi's intention to cut is felt, Fumio Manaka dives forward to avoid the grandmaster's *shinku giri* lateral sword slash. Note Masaaki Hatsumi's closed eyes; Fumio Manaka cannot rely on the grandmaster to stop his sword if there is any hesitation on Manaka's part.

The Power of Kuji

Vastly misunderstood by the popular press responsible for the ninja movies, novels, and comic books that influence the public's image of ninjutsu, the concept of *kuji*, or the "nine syllables," remains one of the more exotic and bizzare skills of the fictional ninja. By merely weaving his fingers together in what seems to be impossible knots and mumbling an obscure incantation, the storybook ninja is then enabled to walk across the surface of water, disappear like a ghost, control the movements of his adversaries, or even take the form of a rat or crow.

As is true with so many other aspects of ninjutsu, there is a core of truth buried in the center of the larger body of myth, legend, and superstition surrounding the ninja's art. In reality, the *kuji* power principle stems from the ancient mystical teachings of Northern India and Tibet. Transported along the Silk Road into China over a thousand years ago, the system continued to undergo development until it was introduced to Japan in the years of China's T'ang Dynasty. The method was a part of the esoteric lore that later came to be known as *mikkyo*, or the "secret doctrines."

The *kuji* nine syllables are most often embodied in one of two possible systems. *Kuji-in* "nine syllable seals" are the hand poses that involve intricate patterns of folding the fingers together. *Kuji-kiri*, "nine syllable slashes" are the symbolic power grids cut into the air with the right hand. In graphic form, the *kuji-in* are represented by a series of Northern Indian script characters, and the *kuji-kiri* are seen as a series of patterns with crossed or interweaving lines.

The hand postures and grid cuttings are in actuality only one third of the whole *kuji* concept. They represent the role of the physical body in action, which must be joined by the intellect in action and the will in action in order to produce results. The three elements of thought, word, and deed coordinated and attuned with each other make up the ninja's *kuji* power principle. The system is in reality a method for learning to remove the gap that separates intention from successful action. Once the *kuji* technique is mastered, the ninja then has the power to create physical reality by means of his intention alone. Focused intention becomes completed action itself; cause blends with effect until the distinction fades.

In combat applications, this ability to focus the intention seems to give the ninja power or energy that defies normal physical laws. Not at all magic in reality, the intention focusing method does not create extra energy, but rather removes the limits that usually restrict the amount of energy available to the normal individual. The physical body is capable of doing the technique, the mind understands what has to be done, and the will is un-hesitating and determined that the task will be completed successfully.

Masaaki Hatsumi fold his hands into one of the *kuji-in* hand positions symbolic of the ninja's direction of spiritual intensity towards the accomplishment of his goal.

Togakure ryu ninjutsu shihan master instructors develop their abilities to channel energy and intentions through training in the methods of *kuji-in* hand posturing and *kuji-kiri* protective grid slashing.

Masaaki Hatsumi simultaneously throws two foreign judoka in a demonstration of controlling the center of gravity and channeling the energy and intentions.

Dr. Masaaki Hatsumi uses a sudden contraction and expansion of his physical body and "energy shell" in order to shake off the grasp of six students.